The
Fresh-Milled
Flour
· BREAD BOOK ·

THE COMPLETE GUIDE TO MASTERING
Your Home Mill ᴼᴿ Artisan Sourdough,
Pizza, Croissants ᴬᴺᴰ More

The
Fresh-Milled
Flour
· BREAD BOOK ·

Tim Giuffi
Owner of Lyman Ave. Bread

PAGE STREET
PUBLISHING CO.

PAGE STREET
PUBLISHING CO.

Copyright © 2023 Tim Giuffi

First published in 2023 by
Page Street Publishing Co.
27 Congress Street, Suite 1511
Salem, MA 01970
www.pagestreetpublishing.com

Distributed by Macmillan, sales in Canada by The Canadian Manda Group.

27   26   25   24   23   1   2   3   4   5

ISBN-13: 978-1-64567-959-2
ISBN-10: 1-64567-959-4

Library of Congress Control Number: 2022946941

Cover and book design by Laura Benton for Page Street Publishing Co.

Photography by Josh Darr

Printed and bound in the United States of America

TO NORA AND KRISTA,
FOR THEIR LOVE AND SUPPORT

CONTENTS

INTRODUCTION

My week starts on Sunday at my small cottage bakery just outside of Chicago. I lug a Mockmill® Pro 200 to the table and get ready to mill about 50 pounds of grains into various flours for the week. Luckily, the mill is a workhorse and makes easy work of the milling process. Though loud, I find this part of the process to be the most relaxing. There's just something about taking a whole grain and pulverizing it into a fine flour and being in complete control of the process.

I find baking bread to be a pretty personal experience, especially since I'm doing it solo—no helpers, just me, the flour and the oven. I love getting my hands in the dough, feeling it change over time and delivering the bread directly to my customers. It's hard work, but it's the most fun I've ever had, and I never stop learning.

In this book, you'll find a variety of recipes that showcase fresh-milled grains, both by them-selves, which lets the grains shine, but also with ingredients that complement the flour to make for some delicious bread.

The recipes in this book are scaled down recipes directly from my bakery, and all measurements are done in grams. This is to make sure things remain nice and consistent from bake to bake. Volume measurements like cups and tablespoons are not as accurate, and you can end up with a different product than intended when measuring by volume.

Most of the recipes also utilize a sourdough starter. The depth of flavor that sourdough provides can't be matched and adding in freshly-milled flour simply takes the bread to another level. I feed my sourdough starter daily with sifted bread flour in a ratio of two parts flour, two parts water and one part sourdough starter. It stays at 80°F (27°C) in a small tabletop proofer. Typically, it will take 4 to 6 hours to peak, which is when it should be used in these recipes. Knowing your starter and how it behaves is one of the most important parts of making quality, consistent sourdough bread. So, if you have a starter that you are happy with, it will work just fine in the recipes here.

I'm excited to share my experiences with you and hope you find the recipes in this book to be both helpful and fun to make.

MILLS & HOW TO USE THEM

Milling grains on a commercial scale is surely a science. It's important to have the flour be consistent every time with a large production. Milling grains at home is *not* an exact science. Home mills aren't designed to give you a perfectly consistent product every time. This is a good thing. It allows for more experimentation and opportunities to learn. It's also difficult to know exactly what is being asked for with vague terms like "fine" and "coarse." If your flour is a little different than it was the last time, the dough might handle a little bit differently, but you're still going to end up with great bread!

MILLING GRAINS

I've extensively used two mills—the Mockmill 100 and the Mockmill Pro 200. They both produce amazing flour, with the Mockmill Pro being a little faster. When I'm milling a fine flour, I like to set the mill so I can just hear the stones touching—they'll make a clicking noise. I then add the grains and push the mill as far as I can, until I feel some resistance. The grains will keep the stones separate, but make sure to stand by so when the process is finished you can move the stones apart. This way they don't get damaged. The screeching sound of the stones grinding against each other is not one you want to hear. I don't pay much attention to the numbers on the mill—on the Mockmill Pro there are settings from 0 to 20, which makes it seem like 0 would be the finest, but I've found that when I mill at 0, I end up with more of a fine semolina texture. I push the mill way past the 0 mark to get a fine flour.

When milling very hard grains, especially Kamut and durum, I like to double mill. For double millings, the first pass shouldn't be too fine because the flour will stick together during the second pass, and you'll have to stand there and push it through the hopper. A fine semolina texture is perfect for the first mill so the flour will move readily through the mill during the second pass.

Milling grains more coarsely, as for a semolina texture or a coarse cornmeal, will take some trial and error. It's better to err on the side of too coarse because you can always send the flour through again.

There is some disagreement about how long to let the flour sit before using it in a dough. Some people believe it should be used immediately, and others think it should be rested before using. I've done everything from using the flour right out of the mill to letting the flour sit for a couple of weeks before making dough with it. I have to say, I haven't noticed any huge difference in the performance of the flour.

My preference is to mill the day before I'm going to mix the dough. I do this because I like to split up the workload and to allow the flour to cool to room temperature. This makes it easier for me to know what temperature water I should use for the dough. If you're going to use the flour without a rest period, just be mindful of the flour's temperature.

SIFTING FLOUR

Most recipes in this book call for a sifted bread flour. This is achieved by sifting the whole flour through a 50-mesh sifter. My sifter is a plastic piece of mining equipment that I found on Amazon. It fits perfectly over a five-gallon bucket. I have a few different mesh sizes, but I've found the 50-mesh is the only one I really use, except for a regular kitchen strainer that I use to separate coarse pieces that are too big to use (which can be milled again). The sifted flour will still have some of the germ and bran remaining, and it'll be darker than commercial bread flour. When sifting flour, you can count on about 20 percent loss from the initial weight of the berries. This is mostly from what has been sifted out, but you'll also lose some flour that gets stuck to the sifter. The recipes in this book take that 20 percent loss into account, but it's not exact, so you may need to mill a little more.

WHEAT BRAN AND RICE FLOUR COATING

Make sure to save the wheat bran you sift out. It will be used to coat the bottoms of many breads in this book to insulate them from burning. We'll also make a mixture of wheat bran and rice flour to dust over the towels used for proofing.

To make this mixture, mill 200 grams of white or brown rice to a fine consistency. Add it to a medium sized container (I like to use deli quart containers) and add some wheat bran so you have two parts rice flour and one part bran. Cover the container and shake it together. It'll last for months when kept covered in a cool, dark space.

GRAINS & WHERE TO GET THEM

We're living in a great time for grains. There are many farmers growing an amazing variety of grains, and most of them ship. You can even find berries at your local grocery store, either from Bob's Red Mill® or in the bulk section at some specialty stores. On my last visit to my local co-op, I noticed they were selling wheat, rye, spelt and Kamut berries in the bulk bins, all for a reasonable price.

The best way to source your grains is to find a local farmer. I'm lucky in Chicagoland, because there are several grain farmers. I get most of my grains from Janie's Mill, just south of Chicago. Being able to source locally is not only better for the environment and the local economy, but it'll also save you on shipping costs as well. There is a great resource for sourcing grains by state on the Challenger® Breadware website: www.challengerbreadware.com.

If you're unable to find a local source or are looking for something that doesn't grow locally, Breadtopia® (www.breadtopia.com) is a great resource for grains. They usually have a dozen or so different types available.

In all my years of using whole grains, I've never run across a batch that didn't look pristine, but one problem I have encountered is a storage issue that makes the grains smell almost like cinnamon. The first time this happened to me was with a bag of Turkey Red. I actually kind of enjoyed the smell and the spicy flavor the flour imparted to the bread—until one day I grabbed the bag from my pantry and it was loaded with bugs. It turns out the cinnamon smell is an indication that the grains haven't been stored properly from the farmers or during transportation/distribution. It's a smell I can't forget, and I will toss grain that smells this way.

I organize my stash of grains into the following categories, making it easier to switch out berries with similar profiles.

HARD RED WHEAT: Bold and nutty tasting, hard red wheat berries are the workhorse of bread baking. They have the protein content to provide the backbone for your dough. Hard red spring varieties like Glenn, Bolles and Yecora Rojo will typically have a higher protein content than hard red winter varieties like Turkey Red, Warthog and Red Fife. Keeping both types on hand allows you to combine the grains in different proportions to make the flour exactly as strong as you want it.

SOFT RED WHEAT: Soft red wheat is not high in protein. It is great for pastries or pancakes. It is also useful to bring down the protein content of strong flour to make it a bit softer and easier to work with, such as in the croissant recipes in this book.

HARD WHITE WHEAT: Less intense than their red counterparts, hard white wheat varieties like Pasayten and Edison provide a milder flavor but still have the high protein to make a strong dough. The bread flour used throughout this book includes a mix of both hard red and hard white wheats.

RYE

DURUM WHEAT

GLENN WHEAT

BLOODY
BUTCHER
CORN

KAMUT

SPELT

TURKEY
RED
WHEAT

EINKORN

FREDERICK
WHITE WHEAT

BLUE CORN

SOFT WHITE WHEAT: Lower in protein but packed with flavor, soft white wheat varieties like Frederick or Sonora wheats are great to mix with the higher protein wheats to provide a softer, more tender crumb.

RYE: In a category all to itself, there's nothing else quite like rye. Slightly spicy and grassy, the flavor is unmistakable. Used by itself, it will produce a dough, completely unlike any wheat dough and a bread that is dense and hearty. In a flour mix, its unmistakable flavor will shine, providing depth to the bread.

GOLDEN WHEATS: The beautiful golden flours produced by Kamut and durum berries are some of my favorites. Nutty and buttery with a high protein content, these grains produce a dough that is a pleasure to work with and even more of a pleasure to eat.

Kamut is the registered name of an ancient grain called Khorasan. It shows up on the shelves as Kamut more frequently than as Khorasan, so we'll refer to it as Kamut throughout.

You'll often find durum milled into semolina, which is perfect for pasta, but occasionally you can find sifted durum flour available in some specialty stores.

Both Kamut and durum are very hard, and it is difficult to produce a fine flour with the first pass through the mill, so double milling is recommended.

ANCIENT GRAINS: Flavor bombs all around, einkorn, emmer, and spelt all have a nutty earthiness like no other. Even a small amount in a flour mix will completely change the flavor profile.

Small and packed with nutrients, einkorn is the earliest cultivated wheat. It's high in protein, but its gluten structure differs from modern wheat. When used alone, einkorn will produce a dense hearty loaf that is best suited to pan loaves.

Bold and unique in flavor, emmer, much like einkorn, is one of the earliest cultivated wheats. Mixing a bit into a country dough will add a pop of flavor. Emmer sometimes doesn't mill as easily as einkorn or spelt. In fact, with one type of emmer that I've used in the past, Ethiopian Blue-Tinge emmer, I was unable to ever produce a fine flour, even after double milling.

Nutty and versatile, spelt adds a great flavor and extensibility to any dough. I like to use spelt in doughs that I need to be a little more extensible, like baguettes. Doughs containing spelt can sometimes be a bit difficult to work with due to this extensibility. Quick, confident shaping is necessary.

GRAIN FORWARD
Sourdough Breads Showcasing Whole Grains

If bread making is an art, then grains make up the artist's palette. The flavors, colors and textures are so varied, and the combinations are endless. You can take some typical whole wheat, say Red Fife, mill it up nice and fine and make a bold, nutty loaf of bread. But swap out some of that flour for freshly-milled rye and you'll end up with a completely different loaf of bread. The loaf will vary in color, texture and flavor just by changing a little bit of the flour.

My love affair with grains started at a food swap at my local co-op. Every month, people would gather to trade homemade or homegrown goods. I was just starting to figure out how to bake a larger quantity of bread and used these swaps as a way to practice. I had my mill at this time, but I hadn't really explored many different grains; I was just buying what I could find at the grocery store. One of my fellow swappers told me he would bring in some einkorn the following month. He said that the aroma of freshly-milled einkorn transported him back to his days spent on his family farm in his youth. I was sold and couldn't wait to get my hands on some.

I spent the whole month anticipating the next swap when I would get that einkorn. Sure, I could have ordered some online, but it felt important to wait and trade a loaf of bread with my new friend. As soon as I got home that afternoon, I broke out the mill and turned those tiny little wheat berries into the most beautiful flour. I totally understood why my friend was reminded of a farm. The smell was so rich and earthy. I've been hooked ever since.

I immediately scoured the internet to order any grain I could get my hands on and have never looked back. My palette has been full ever since.

I call the recipes in this chapter Grain Forward because the only ingredients used are grains in different textures, from the finest flour to completely whole, plus water and salt. There are five different country-style sourdoughs to start, and they really showcase the difference between the grains. They're all pretty much the same recipe but swapping out the whole grain portion makes an entirely different bread. A few pan loaves round it out, from hearty and dense like the Einkorn & Rye Pan Loaf (page 36), to my absolute favorite sandwich bread made with scalded durum (page 39).

WHOLE WHEAT & RYE COUNTRY SOURDOUGH

YIELDS ONE LOAF, ABOUT 750 GRAMS

This is it: The loaf of bread that I've spent the last ten years or so working on. Every week, I make a few dozen of these loaves for my farmers' market stand, and every week I'm amazed at how something so simple can be so complex at the same time. Like a Grateful Dead concert, it's pretty much the same yet entirely different every time.

This is the basic country loaf, mostly sifted bread flour with a bit of whole wheat and whole rye flours. Hard red spring and hard white spring wheat berries are used both sifted and unsifted in the bread.

Whether this is your first home-milled loaf or you've been milling your own flour for a while, this recipe will provide the backbone for the techniques used throughout the book. So, jump in and have fun!

---

350 grams wheat berry blend for 280 grams sifted bread flour

40 grams Glenn wheat berries

30 grams hard white spring wheat berries

20 grams rye berries

74 grams active sourdough starter

296 grams water, divided

8 grams kosher salt

Wheat bran and rice flour mixture, for the basket (see page 12)

Wheat bran, for coating the bottom

FOR THE WHEAT BERRY BLEND: This wheat blend consists of equal parts high protein red wheat and hard white spring wheat and is the perfect blend for bread flour. The high protein red wheat (I use Glenn wheat because it is readily available to me, but any high protein wheat like Yecora Rojo or Rouge de Bordeaux will work just fine) adds a full flavor and structure to the dough. The hard white spring wheat (I use Pasayten, but any hard white spring wheat such as Edison will do) tempers the robust flavor of the hard red wheat and brings down the protein content a bit, making a more tender loaf.

This flour blend is called for in most recipes in this book. If you know you're going to be using it, it wouldn't hurt to mill a larger batch and keep the flour in an airtight container for a week or two rather than milling it to order every time.

FOR THE FLOUR: Mill the wheat berry blend as fine as you can, sift it through a 50-mesh sifter and measure out 280 grams of sifted flour into a large bowl. Save the wheat bran for both the rice flour mixture for the basket and to coat the bottom of the loaf.

In a medium bowl, mix the Glenn, hard white spring and rye berries. Mill them as fine as you can, and add the milled flour straight to the bowl with the bread flour without sifting. Mix well.

(continued)

Whole Wheat & Rye Country Sourdough (Continued)

MIXING: In a large bowl with a lid, dissolve the sourdough starter in 288 grams of water. Temperature is really important at this stage, and the easiest ingredient to control is the water. In the dead of winter, you're going to want to use warmer water than you would in the heat of the summer.

For example, my flour is typically around 60°F (16°C) in the winter because I keep it in my basement. Since the room is 60°F (16°C), I shoot for a higher dough temperature of 84°F (29°C) because the temperature of the dough will drop quickly, and the higher temperature will get the dough moving. In order to achieve a dough temperature of 84°F (29°C), I use water that is about 104°F (40°C). Taking the dough higher than 84°F (29°C) can have a negative effect, especially when using fresh flour, so take care not to go higher than that.

On the other end of the spectrum, in the middle of the summer, my flour and room temperature are closer to 75°F (24°C), so I want a lower dough temperature of 78 to 80°F (26 to 27°C). In order to achieve this, I use water that is 78 to 80°F (26 to 27°C).

After dissolving the sourdough starter in the water, mix in the flour until it is incorporated, and no dry flour remains. To this day, though I make a couple of hundred loaves a week, I mix everything by hand. I really enjoy getting my hands in the dough and being able to feel how it changes over time. It's a great way to learn the dough and to figure out if it needs a little more water or a little more development.

Cover the bowl with the lid (if your bowl doesn't have a lid, use a plastic bag), and allow the dough to rest for about an hour. This will provide the flour time to absorb the water and gain some strength.

After resting for an hour, add the salt and remaining 8 grams of water to the dough. Squeeze it in until the salt is fully dissolved. You'll be able to feel if there is any salt remaining. At this point, if the dough feels a little stiff, you can add more water, a little at a time, until the desired consistency is reached. Cover and let the dough rest for 30 minutes.

STRETCH AND FOLD METHOD

FOLDS & BULK FERMENTATION: After the 30-minute rest period, it is time to perform the first set of stretch and folds. Place a small bowl with water on your workstation. Dipping your hands in the water before touching the dough will ensure that the dough doesn't stick to your hands. Since we didn't really develop the dough in the initial mix, these stretch and folds will provide the necessary strength and gluten development.

Take one side of the dough, stretch it up, and fold it to the middle. Turn the bowl 90 degrees and repeat, until you've folded all four sides. Cover the bowl and allow to rest for another 30 minutes, repeating the stretch and folds twice more for a total of three stretch and folds. The dough needs to relax in between folds or else you risk tearing it. Usually, 30 minutes is the right amount of time for the dough to rest. If the dough looks like it's still tense from the previous fold, let it rest 10 extra minutes before the next fold.

After the last fold, allow the dough to rest, covered, for about 2 more hours. Of course, this amount of time is totally dependent on the temperature of the room and of the dough. Watching the dough is more important than watching the clock. The dough should be significantly airier than it was during the last fold—almost like a winter coat. A 50 percent rise in volume is about where it should be, and it should be releasing from the sides of the bowl. A well-fermented dough is not as sticky as an under-fermented dough, and it will release easily from the bowl, even without oil.

(continued)

PRESHAPE METHOD

SHAPING METHOD FOR BATARD

PRESHAPE: When bulk fermentation is complete, it is time to preshape the dough. This can seem like an unnecessary step when you're only making one loaf of bread, but it will make shaping a whole lot easier.

Remove the dough from the bowl—it should just slide right out—and place it on an un-floured work surface. Using a bench knife, form the dough into a round, and allow it to rest for about an hour. If your room is dry, you can cover the dough with a towel to prevent a film from forming, but if it's humid, covering is unnecessary. Resting the dough for an hour will allow it to relax and ferment a little bit longer. This makes shaping easier and more consistent.

SHAPING: Line a proofing basket with a towel, and coat the towel in the rice flour mixture.

Lightly flour a work surface—you don't want too much, or the dough will have trouble sticking to itself. With your bench knife, flip the dough over onto the flour. I like to shape country sourdoughs into oval shapes, but if you want a round, go for it. To shape into an oval, fold the top of the dough about two-thirds of the way down, and fold the bottom of the dough about two-thirds of the way up so they overlap a little. Turn the dough 90 degrees and roll it up from the top down. Place in the prepared basket, seam side up, and coat the bottom of the dough (the seam side that's facing up in the basket) with wheat bran. The wheat bran will provide a layer of insulation to the bottom of the loaf, keeping it from burning.

PROOFING: Allow the dough to rest at room temperature for 1 to 2 hours, depending on the temperature—both of the room and of the fridge you will place the dough in overnight. You'll want to see about a 20 percent rise before putting it in the fridge. In the dead of winter, when my basement is 60°F (16°C), I have a lot of flexibility with this initial room temperature rest—it can go as long as 5 hours. In the summer, I sometimes have to skip the rest altogether and go straight to the fridge. Learning your dough is the most important part here.

Place the dough in the fridge overnight. Fridge temperatures can vary significantly, even within the fridge itself, so if you put the dough in a warmer spot, it'll proof quicker than if you put it in the back of the fridge near the fan.

BAKING: There are two ways to bake loaves in a home oven: with a Dutch oven or with a pizza stone and a tray of lava rocks to provide steam. I prefer the Dutch oven when the bread I'm making will fit, but that's not always the case.

To bake in a Dutch oven, place the Dutch oven into your oven and preheat it to 500°F (260°C) for at least an hour so the Dutch oven can get nice and hot. I've baked in several different ovens, and they vary considerably in how hot they get. My current oven is perfect at 500°F (260°C), but with my previous oven I needed to bake at 550°F (288°C).

In the meantime, take your dough out of the fridge and allow it to rest at room temperature while the oven preheats. This will loosen it up and take some of the chill off.

When the Dutch oven is nice and hot, flip the dough onto a piece of parchment paper and score it with one quick slash, right down the middle. Remove the Dutch oven from the oven and use the parchment as a sling to transfer the dough to the Dutch oven. Cover it with the lid and place it back in the oven. Bake with the lid on for 20 minutes, then remove the lid and the parchment paper because the overhanging parchment that was used as a sling can burn. Bake the loaf for another 20 to 25 minutes until it reaches the desired color. I prefer a very bold bake on these country sourdoughs, as I think it brings out the full potential and flavor of the grains. It's worth noting that if your bread is perfectly proofed, it will color differently than if it is slightly under- or over-proofed. I find under- and over-proofed doughs will burn more readily than a dough that proofed right. A perfectly proofed dough will color more evenly, so you can push it a bit further.

Remove the bread from the Dutch oven and place it on a wire rack to cool.

To bake with a pizza stone and lava rocks, place the stone on the middle rack of your oven (I actually never take my pizza stone out of the oven—it's heavy). Put the lava rocks in a cast-iron skillet and put that on the oven floor. Preheat the oven to 500°F (260°C) for at least 1 hour so everything gets really hot. In the meantime, boil about 2 cups (473 ml) of water.

When it's time to bake, flip the dough onto a piece of parchment paper and score it. Using a pizza peel, slide the dough onto the stone. Very carefully pour the boiling water over the lava rocks. And I mean *very carefully*—they're crazy hot, and if you splash some water on the glass of your oven door, there is a chance it could shatter. Placing a towel over the glass while you're pouring the water can prevent this from happening.

Bake with steam for 20 minutes. After 20 minutes, remove the skillet with the lava rocks and bake the bread for an additional 20 minutes or so, until the desired color is reached. When finished, place the loaf on a wire rack to cool for a couple of hours.

THE SAD CASE OF A BURNT BOTTOM

We've all been there. You spent two days working on a loaf of sourdough bread. You fed your starter three times before using it, milled and sifted all your flour, mixed the dough and spent hours watching it. You shaped it perfectly and nailed the proof. For the first time, your score opened up exactly how you pictured it. But after 40 minutes on a hot piece of cast iron, the bottom of your bread is scorched. Of course, if you're like me, you'll try to convince yourself that it's fine, the bottom should be a little darker than the rest. But deep down you know it's burnt.

To compensate for this, you might try lowering the oven temperature next time. That would make sense, but the high heat is necessary to get that perfect spring. A simple solution for these burnt bottoms is to place a rack under the loaf after you remove the lid. This raises the bottom of the bread off the hot metal. If you don't have a rack that fits inside of the Dutch oven, you can take the entire loaf out and put it on a rack placed in a sheet tray for the rest of the bake.

COUNTRY SOURDOUGH WITH SPELT FLOUR

YIELDS ONE LOAF, ABOUT 750 GRAMS

Spelt has a nuttiness that can't be beat. When using a higher proportion of spelt flour, like the 30 percent in this recipe, I like to cut back the water just a little bit. Spelt can make the dough somewhat difficult to handle, especially if it is too wet.

325 grams wheat berry blend for 260 grams sifted
   bread flour

115 grams spelt berries

76 grams active sourdough starter

280 grams water, divided

8 grams kosher salt

Wheat bran and rice flour mixture, for the basket
   (see page 12)

Wheat bran, for coating the bottom

FOR THE FLOUR: Mill the wheat berries as fine as you can and sift through a 50-mesh sifter. Measure out 260 grams of flour, and place it in a medium sized bowl. Save the wheat bran to coat the bottom of the dough after shaping.

Mill the spelt berries as fine as possible and add to the bowl with the sifted flour.

MIXING: In a large bowl with a lid, dissolve the sourdough starter in 272 grams of water. Add the flour and mix everything by hand until there is no more dry flour. Cover with the lid and rest for 1 hour. After resting, squeeze in the salt and the remaining 8 grams of water until both are fully incorporated. Rest, covered, for 30 minutes.

BULK FERMENTATION: After resting for 30 minutes, give the dough one round of stretch and folds. Repeat this step twice more. After the last stretch and fold, bulk fermentation will last 2 to 2½ more hours until the dough has risen by about 50 percent and feels airy. The dough should remain covered the entire time.

PRESHAPE: Remove the dough from the container onto an un-floured work surface. Using a bench knife, shape the dough into a round. Rest for 45 to 60 minutes until the dough is relaxed.

SHAPING: Line a proofing basket with a towel and coat with rice flour and wheat bran mixture.

Shape the dough into an oval. Place it seam side up in the prepared basket, coat the bottom with wheat bran, and cover the basket with a plastic bag.

PROOFING & BAKING: Proof the dough for 1 to 2 hours at room temperature until the dough has loosened and risen by about 20 percent before placing it in the fridge overnight.

The next day, place a Dutch oven in your oven and preheat to 500°F (260°C) for about an hour to make sure the Dutch oven is nice and hot. Remove the dough from the fridge and allow it to rest at room temperature while the oven preheats to get some of the chill off. Score the dough and place it in the Dutch oven. Bake with the lid on for 20 minutes, then remove the lid and bake for 20 more minutes until it is dark and toasty. When finished, place the loaf on a wire rack to cool for a couple of hours.

KAMUT, DURUM & FREDERICK WHITE WHEAT COUNTRY SOURDOUGH

YIELDS ONE LOAF, ABOUT 750 GRAMS

This is my go-to loaf when I want to show someone how amazing and complex a loaf of bread can be. The golden wheats Kamut and durum add such a nice buttery flavor and chewy texture, which is tempered by the softness of the Frederick wheat. This loaf benefits from a deep, bold bake. Don't be afraid to push it.

---

325 grams wheat berry blend for 260 grams sifted bread flour

45 grams Kamut berries

45 grams durum berries

25 grams Frederick white wheat berries

76 grams active sourdough starter

300 grams water, divided

8 grams kosher salt

Wheat bran and rice flour mixture, for the basket (see page 12)

Wheat bran, for coating the bottom

FOR THE FLOUR: Mill the wheat berries as fine as you can and sift through a 50-mesh sifter. Measure out 260 grams of flour, and place it in a medium sized bowl. Save the wheat bran to coat the bottom of the dough after shaping.

In a medium bowl, mix the Kamut and durum berries, and mill them as finely as you can (they will still feel a little sandy). Add the whole Frederick white wheat berries to the Kamut and durum flour, and pass it through the mill again, milling it as fine as possible. Add this to the bowl with the sifted bread flour and mix well.

MIXING: In a large bowl with a lid, dissolve the sourdough starter in 292 grams of water. Add the flour and mix everything by hand until there is no more dry flour. Cover with the lid and rest for 1 hour. After resting for an hour, squeeze in the salt and remaining 8 grams of water until they are fully incorporated. Rest, covered, for 30 minutes.

BULK FERMENTATION: After resting for 30 minutes, give the dough one round of stretch and folds. Repeat this step twice more. After the last stretch and fold, bulk fermentation will last 2 to 2½ more hours until the dough has risen by about 50 percent and feels airy. The dough should remain covered the entire time.

PRESHAPE: Remove the dough from the container onto an un-floured work surface. Using a bench knife, shape the dough into a round. Rest for 45 to 60 minutes until the dough is relaxed.

SHAPING: Line a proofing basket with a towel, and coat it with rice flour and wheat bran mixture.

Shape the dough into an oval. Place it seam-side up in the prepared basket, then coat the bottom with wheat bran, and cover it with a plastic bag.

PROOFING & BAKING: Proof the dough for 1 to 2 hours at room temperature until the dough has loosened and risen by about 20 percent before placing it in the fridge overnight.

The next day, place a Dutch oven in your oven and preheat to 500°F (260°C) for about an hour to make sure the Dutch oven is nice and hot. Remove the dough from the fridge, and allow it to rest at room temperature while the oven preheats to get some of the chill off. Score the dough and place it in the Dutch oven. Bake the bread with the lid on for 20 minutes, then remove the lid and bake for 20 more minutes until it is dark and toasty. When finished, place the loaf on a wire rack to cool for a couple of hours.

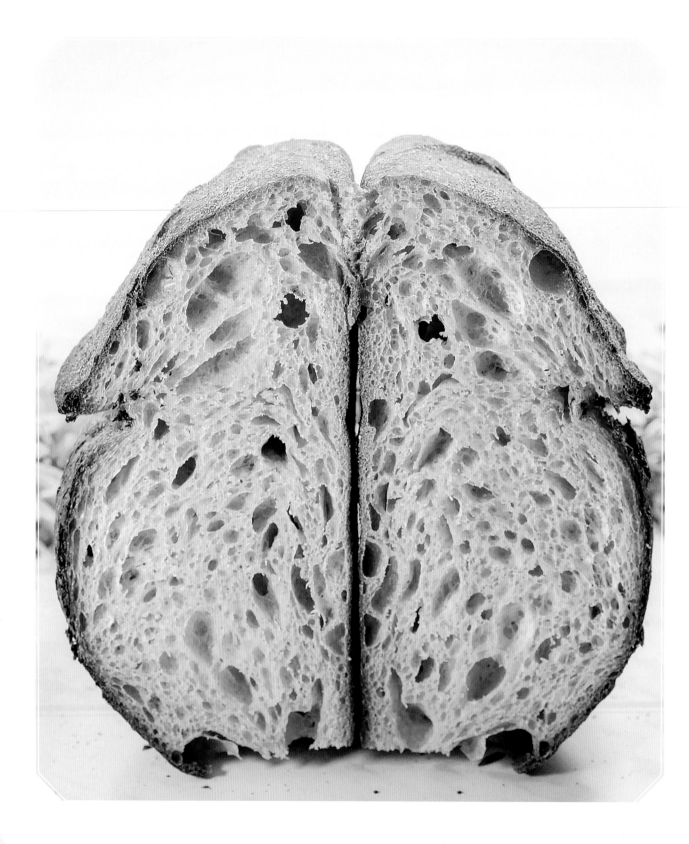

EINKORN, EMMER & SPELT COUNTRY SOURDOUGH

In Italy, einkorn, emmer and spelt are all referred to as farro piccolo, farro medio, and farro grande, respectively. When I learned this, I couldn't resist the urge to add the three of them together to a loaf of country sourdough. If I were one to name my breads with cutesy names, I would call this one Three Farros. All three grains have huge, nutty flavors that really shine in this loaf.

325 grams wheat berry blend for 260 grams sifted bread flour

38 grams einkorn berries

38 grams emmer berries

38 grams spelt berries

76 grams active sourdough starter

300 grams water, divided

8 grams kosher salt

Wheat bran and rice flour mixture, for the basket (see page 12)

Wheat bran, for coating the bottom

FOR THE FLOUR: Mill the wheat berries as fine as you can and sift through a 50-mesh sifter. Measure out 260 grams of flour, and place it in a large sized bowl. Save the wheat bran to coat the bottom of the dough after shaping.

In a medium bowl, mix the einkorn, emmer and spelt berries, and mill them as fine as you can. Add this to the bowl with the sifted bread flour and mix well.

MIXING: In a large bowl with a lid, dissolve the sourdough starter in 292 grams of water. Add the flour and mix everything by hand until there is no more dry flour. Cover the bowl with the lid and rest for 1 hour. After resting for an hour squeeze in the salt and remaining 8 grams of water until both are fully incorporated. Rest, covered, for 30 minutes.

BULK FERMENTATION: After resting for 30 minutes, give the dough one round of stretch and folds. Repeat this step twice more. After the last stretch and fold, bulk fermentation will last 2 to 2½ hours until the dough has risen by about 50 percent and feels airy. The dough should remain covered the entire time.

PRESHAPE: Remove the dough from the container, and place it onto an un-floured work surface. Using a bench knife, shape the dough into a round. Rest for 45 to 60 minutes until the dough is relaxed.

SHAPING: Line a proofing basket with a towel, and coat it with the rice flour and wheat bran mixture.

Shape the dough into an oval. Place it seam-side up in the prepared basket, coat the bottom in wheat bran and cover the basket with a plastic bag.

PROOFING & BAKING: Proof the dough for 1 to 2 hours at room temperature until the dough has loosened and risen by about 20 percent before placing it in the fridge overnight.

The next day, place a Dutch oven in your oven and preheat to 500°F (260°C) for about an hour to make sure the Dutch oven is nice and hot. Remove the dough from the fridge, and allow it to rest at room temperature while the oven preheats to get some of the chill off. Score the dough, and place it in the Dutch oven. Bake with the lid on for 20 minutes, then remove the lid and bake for 20 more minutes until it is dark and toasty. When finished, place the loaf on a wire rack to cool for a couple of hours.

A BLEND OF HARD WHITE SPRING & SONORA WHITE WHEATS

YIELDS ONE LOAF, ABOUT 750 GRAMS

When I first started selling bread, I would often have people ask me if I ever made plain white bread. This recipe was as much of a compromise as I was willing to make. Being a blend of hard and soft white wheats, it's a little milder in flavor, but the fresh-milled flour elevates it to something special. The hard white spring berries are used both sifted as the base flour and unsifted to add some extra flavor.

383 grams hard white spring wheat berries, divided

58 grams Sonora white wheat berries

76 grams active sourdough starter

300 grams water, divided

8 grams kosher salt

Wheat bran and rice flour mixture, for the basket (see page 12)

Wheat bran, for coating the bottom

FOR THE FLOUR: Measure out 325 grams of hard white spring wheat berries, mill them as fine as you can and sift through a 50-mesh sifter. Measure out 260 grams of flour, and add it to a large bowl. Save the wheat bran to coat the bottom of the dough after shaping.

In a medium bowl, mix the remaining 58 grams of hard white spring berries and the 58 grams of Sonora berries and mill them fine as you can. Add this to the bowl with the sifted bread flour and mix well.

MIXING: In a large bowl with a lid, dissolve the sourdough starter in 292 grams of water. Add the flour and mix everything by hand until there is no more dry flour. Cover the bowl with the lid and rest for 1 hour. After resting for an hour, squeeze in the salt and the remaining 8 grams of water until both are fully incorporated. Let the dough rest, covered, for 30 minutes.

BULK FERMENTATION: After resting for 30 minutes, give the dough one round of stretch and folds. Repeat this step twice more. After the last stretch and fold, bulk fermentation will last 2 to 2½ more hours until the dough has risen by about 50 percent and feels airy. The dough should remain covered the entire time.

PRESHAPE: Remove the dough from the container onto an un-floured work surface. Using a bench knife, shape the dough into a round. Rest for 45 to 60 minutes until the dough is relaxed.

SHAPING: Line a proofing basket with a towel, and coat it with the rice flour and wheat bran mixture.

Shape the dough into an oval. Place it seam side up in the prepared basket, coat the bottom with wheat bran and cover the basket with a plastic bag.

PROOFING & BAKING: Proof the dough for 1 to 2 hours at room temperature until the dough has loosened and risen by about 20 percent before placing it in the fridge overnight.

The next day, place a Dutch oven in your oven and preheat to 500°F (260°C) for about an hour to make sure the Dutch oven is nice and hot. Remove the dough from the fridge, and allow it to rest at room temperature while the oven preheats to get some of the chill off. Score the dough and place it in the Dutch oven. Bake with the lid on for 20 minutes, remove the lid and bake for 20 more minutes until it is dark and toasty. When finished, place the loaf on a wire rack to cool for a couple of hours.

HALF WHOLE WHEAT BOULE WITH RED FIFE

YIELDS ONE LOAF, ABOUT 800 GRAMS

A trade-off happens when you add a larger quantity of whole grains to your dough. The bread becomes a little denser, perhaps not as tall and the crumb isn't as open, but the flavor of the whole grain completely makes up for all that. When I'm baking for my family at home, I gravitate toward using 50 percent whole wheat. You can still get the versatile qualities of a country bread but with the added flavor and health benefits from using more whole grain. Red Fife is the perfect variety for this. It has a bold, nutty flavor and handles well when used in higher quantities.

---

250 grams wheat berry blend for 200 grams sifted bread flour

200 grams Red Fife berries

80 grams active sourdough starter

328 grams water, divided

9 grams kosher salt

Wheat bran and rice flour mixture, for the basket (see page 12)

Wheat bran, for coating the bottom

FOR THE FLOUR: Mill the wheat berries as fine as you can and sift through a 50-mesh sifter. Measure out 200 grams of flour and place in a medium sized bowl.

Mill the Red Fife berries as fine as possible, and add them to the bowl with the sifted flour.

MIXING: In a large bowl with a lid, dissolve the sourdough starter in 319 grams of water. Add the flour and mix everything by hand until there is no more dry flour. Cover with the lid and rest for 1 hour. After resting for an hour, squeeze in the salt and the remaining 9 grams of water until both are fully incorporated. Rest, covered, for 30 minutes.

BULK FERMENTATION: After resting for 30 minutes, give the dough one round of stretch and folds. Repeat this step twice more. After the last stretch and fold, bulk fermentation will last 2 to 2½ more hours until the dough has risen by about 50 percent and feels airy. The dough should remain covered the entire time.

PRESHAPE: Remove the dough from the container, and place it onto an un-floured work surface. Using a bench knife, shape the dough into a round. Rest for 45 to 60 minutes until the dough is relaxed.

SHAPING: Line a proofing basket with a towel, and coat it with the wheat bran and rice flour mixture. Shape the dough into a boule. Place it seam side up in the prepared basket, coat the bottom with wheat bran and cover the basket with a plastic bag.

PROOFING & BAKING: Proof the dough for 1 to 2 hours at room temperature until the dough has loosened and risen by about 20 percent before placing it in the fridge overnight.

The next day, place a Dutch oven in your oven and preheat to 500°F (260°C) for about an hour to make sure the Dutch oven is nice and hot. Remove the dough from the fridge, and allow it to rest at room temperature while the oven preheats to get some of the chill off. Score the dough, and place it in the Dutch oven. Bake it with the lid on for 20 minutes, then remove the lid and bake for 20 more minutes until it is dark and toasty. When finished, place the loaf on a wire rack to cool for a couple of hours.

SHAPING METHOD FOR BOULE

MULTIGRAIN PAN LOAF

YIELDS ONE 9 X 4 X 4–INCH (23 X 10 X 10–CM) PULLMAN LOAF,
ABOUT 1,000 GRAMS

A fan favorite, I can't make enough of this bread when I bring it to the farmers' market. There's so much wonderful textural variation due to the different grains used in the soaker. It also makes for a very moist loaf that is begging to be toasted. You can mix up the grains used in the soaker by adding in a different cracked berry or flaked grain. Cooked brown or wild rice would also be a nice addition. Just be sure to keep the total quantity of grains the same.

FOR THE MULTIGRAIN SOAKER

20 grams corn kernels

20 grams wheat berries

40 grams millet

20 grams rolled oats

10 grams whole buckwheat groats

110 grams boiling water

FOR THE DOUGH

400 grams wheat berry blend for 320 grams sifted bread flour

40 grams rye berries

40 grams spelt berries

80 grams active sourdough starter

280 grams water, divided

9 grams kosher salt

Rolled oats, for coating

FOR THE MULTIGRAIN SOAKER: Mill the corn kernels through a coarse setting on your mill and place in a large bowl with a lid. Using a very coarse setting on the mill, crack the wheat berries so they're in relatively large pieces. Add to the bowl with the cornmeal. Combine the rest of the grains with the cornmeal and cracked wheat, then carefully pour the boiling water over it and mix well. Cover the bowl and allow it to rest for 4 to 12 hours for the grains to absorb the water and soften.

FOR THE FLOUR: Mill the wheat berries as fine as you can and sift through a 50-mesh sifter. Measure out 320 grams of flour, and place it in a large sized bowl.

In a medium bowl, mix the rye berries and spelt berries. Mill this as fine as you can, and add them to the bowl with the sifted flour. Mix well.

MIXING & BULK FERMENTATION: In a large bowl with a lid, dissolve the sourdough starter in 272 grams of water. Add the flour and mix everything by hand until there is no more dry flour. Cover with the lid and rest for 1 hour. After resting for an hour, squeeze in the salt and remaining 8 grams of water. Rest, covered, for 30 minutes.

After resting the dough for 30 minutes, add the multigrain mixture. Place about a fifth of the mixture on the dough, fold over one side and add another fifth of the mixture. Repeat this, adding a fifth of the mixture each time, until you've folded all four sides and added all the multigrain mixture.

Rest 30 minutes and perform another series of stretch and folds. Repeat this step once more for a total of three stretch and folds. Bulk fermentation will last about 2½ to 3 hours after the last stretch and fold. Keep the dough covered the entire time. It is ready for preshaping when it has risen by about 50 percent and feels airy.

34 THE FRESH-MILLED FLOUR BREAD BOOK

PRESHAPE: Remove the dough from the container onto an un-floured work surface and use a bench knife to shape the dough into a round. Rest for 45 to 60 minutes for the dough to relax. In the meantime, place the rolled oats in a large bowl.

SHAPING: Lightly oil a 9 × 4 × 4–inch (23 × 10 × 10–cm) Pullman pan. Fold a kitchen towel in half, wet it and wring it out so it is slightly moist.

COATING THE DOUGH

On a lightly floured surface, shape the dough into a log. Roll the entire dough on the wet towel then place it in the bowl with the oats. Coat the whole thing, top and bottom, with the oats. Place it seam side down in the prepared pan and cover the pan with a plastic bag.

PROOFING & BAKING: Proof the dough for 1 to 2 hours at room temperature until the dough has risen by about 20 percent, then place it in the fridge overnight.

The next day, set up your oven for steaming with lava rocks. Preheat the oven to 450°F (232°C). Meanwhile, remove the dough from the fridge so it can loosen up and get some of the chill off. The dough is ready to be baked when it has risen to just below the top of the pan.

Score the dough if desired, place the pan in the oven and carefully pour boiling water over the lava rocks to create steam. Lower the oven to 400°F (204°C) and bake for 20 minutes. Remove the steam and bake for an additional 25 minutes, until the loaf has an internal temperature of at least 190°F (88°C) and is nicely browned. When finished, place the loaf on a wire rack to cool for a couple of hours.

EINKORN & RYE PAN LOAF

YIELDS ONE 9 X 4 X 4–INCH (23 X 10 X 10–CM) PULLMAN LOAF, ABOUT 1,000 GRAMS

This bread is inspired by my friend Jim, who specializes in whole grain pan loaves. His delicious, creative breads always inspire me to push my whole grain baking a little further. Here, we're using the wheat berry blend unsifted, making for a denser loaf of bread. The flavor of einkorn and rye really shine in this hearty pan loaf. The soaker adds a nice textural element to the finished product. It's perfect sliced thin and topped with some smoked fish.

FOR THE SOAKER

60 grams einkorn berries

60 grams rye berries

120 grams boiling water

FOR THE DOUGH

300 grams wheat berry blend for 240 grams sifted bread flour

80 grams einkorn berries

80 grams rye berries

80 grams active sourdough starter

300 grams water, divided

9 grams kosher salt

FOR THE SOAKER: In a small bowl, combine the einkorn and rye berries. Using a coarse setting on your mill, pass the berries through to just crack them. Since the einkorn berries are small, some of them won't crack. That is fine.

Place the cracked berries in a medium bowl with a lid, and carefully pour the boiling water over them. Mix well, cover the bowl and allow to rest for 4 to 12 hours until the berries have absorbed the water and softened a bit.

FOR THE FLOUR: In a medium bowl, combine the wheat berries with the einkorn and rye berries. Mix well. Mill as fine as you can.

MIXING & BULK FERMENTATION: In a large bowl with a lid, dissolve the sourdough starter in 292 grams of water. Add the flour and mix everything by hand until there is no more dry flour. Cover with the lid and rest for 1 hour. After resting for an hour, squeeze in the salt and remaining 8 grams of water. Rest, covered, for 30 minutes.

After resting the dough for 30 minutes, perform the first set of stretch and folds while adding the einkorn and rye soaker. Place about a fifth of the soaker on the dough, fold over one side and add another fifth of the soaker. Fold over another side and add another fifth of the soaker until you've folded all four sides and added all the einkorn and rye soaker.

Allow the dough to rest for 30 minutes, and then perform another series of stretch and folds. Repeat this step once more for a total of three stretch and folds. Bulk fermentation will last about 2½ to 3 hours after the last stretch and fold. Keep the dough covered the entire time. It is ready for preshaping when it has risen by about 50 percent and feels airy.

PRESHAPE: Remove the dough from the container onto an un-floured work surface and use a bench knife to shape the dough into a round. Rest for 45 to 60 minutes to allow the dough to relax.

SHAPING: Lightly oil a 9 × 4 × 4–inch (23 × 10 × 10–cm) Pullman pan.

On a lightly floured surface, shape the dough into a log. Place the dough seam side down in the prepared pan and cover the pan with a plastic bag.

PROOFING & BAKING: Proof the dough for 1 to 2 hours at room temperature until the dough has risen by about 20 percent, then place it in the fridge overnight.

The next day, set up your oven for steaming with lava rocks. Preheat the oven to 450°F (232°C). Meanwhile, remove the dough from the fridge so it can loosen up and get some of the chill off.

Score the dough if desired, place the pan in the oven and carefully pour boiling water over the lava rocks to create steam. Lower the oven to 400°F (204°C) and bake for about 20 minutes. Remove the steam and bake for an additional 25 minutes until the loaf has an internal temperature of at least 190°F (88°C) and is nicely browned. When finished, place the loaf on a wire rack to cool for a couple of hours.

SCALDED DURUM SANDWICH BREAD

YIELDS ONE PAN LOAF, ABOUT 1,150 GRAMS

Imagine a loaf of bread so soft and sweet, perfect for toast and grilled cheeses, but with no added sugars or fats. That's what this bread brings to the table. Making a soaker with coarse durum flour brings out the sweetness of the grain and adds a softness to the crumb. We're using mostly bread flour for the lightness with just a little rye to increase the complexity.

When making a pan bread, I like to push the proof as far as I can so there is no need to score the dough before baking. If it is properly proofed, it won't tear in the oven, and the top will be nice and smooth. This allows for nice, consistent slices for sandwiches.

FOR THE DURUM SOAKER

125 grams durum berries

100 grams boiling water

FOR THE DOUGH

563 grams wheat berry blend for 450 grams sifted bread flour

25 grams rye berries

100 grams active sourdough starter

12 grams kosher salt

375 grams water

FOR THE DURUM SOAKER: Mill the durum berries to a coarse consistency. Sift through a 50-mesh sifter. Place the sifted durum flour in a medium bowl and set it aside. In another medium bowl, place the coarse durum flour left in the sifter, pour over the boiling water and mix well. Cover the bowl and rest for at least 4 hours for the flour to absorb the water and soften.

FOR THE FLOUR: Mill the wheat berries as fine as you can and sift through a 50-mesh sifter. Measure out 450 grams of sifted flour and place in the bowl with the sifted durum flour.

Mill the rye berries as fine as you can, and add them to the bowl with the sifted flours. Mix well.

MIXING & BULK FERMENTATION: In a large bowl with a lid, dissolve the sourdough starter and salt in the water. Add the durum soaker and mix well. Add the flour and mix everything by hand until there is no more dry flour. Cover with the lid and rest for 30 minutes.

After 30 minutes, perform the first set of stretch and folds, cover again and rest 30 more minutes. Repeat this step twice more for a total of three stretch and folds. Bulk fermentation will last about 4 hours after the last stretch and fold, until the dough has doubled and feels thick and airy.

PRESHAPE: Remove the dough from the container onto an un-floured work surface and use a bench knife to shape the dough into a round. Rest for 45 to 60 minutes for the dough to relax.

SHAPING: Lightly oil a 9 × 4 × 4–inch (23 × 10 × 10–cm) Pullman pan.

On a lightly floured surface, shape the dough into a log. Place it seam side down in the prepared pan, and cover the pan with a plastic bag.

PROOFING & BAKING: Proof the dough for 1 to 2 hours at room temperature until the dough has risen by about 20 percent, then place it in the fridge overnight.

The next day, set up your oven for steam with lava rocks. Preheat the oven to 450°F (232°C). Meanwhile, remove the dough from the fridge so it can loosen up and get some of the chill off. The dough is ready to be baked when it has risen to just below the top of the pan.

Stencil if desired, place the pan in the oven and carefully pour boiling water over the lava rocks to create steam. Lower the oven to 400°F (204°C) and bake for about 20 minutes; remove the steam and bake for an additional 25 minutes, until the loaf has an internal temperature of at least 190°F (88°C) and is nicely browned. When finished, place the loaf on a wire rack to cool for a couple of hours.

RUSTIC FIELD BLEND LOAF

YIELDS ONE LOAF, ABOUT 1,000 GRAMS

I keep a wide variety of whole grains on hand, and I try my best to use them at the same rate so when it comes time to buy more, I can restock the entire pantry rather than just a couple at a time. Of course, this means that toward the end, I'm left with small amounts of everything, and it just makes sense to mix them all together. Back when I would keep my grains in the freezer, I would call this bread "Freezer Blend" but since I no longer have the freezer space for the amount of grain I keep, I've changed the name to "Field Blend." Although, I don't know if there's a field anywhere growing such a variety!

I've made this bread with every grain imaginable and haven't really run across a combination that doesn't work. I always have a few varieties of whole wheat, along with rye, einkorn, Kamut, spelt and corn, and that's what I used for the recipe below. In this recipe, the hard red and hard white wheats in the wheat berry blend make up the sifted flour portion, while the rye, ancient grains and corn make up the whole grain portion. But use whatever you've got, and it's going to be great.

Using what's on hand is a pretty rustic idea to me, so I like to make a pretty rustic bread with a higher percentage of whole grain. We're not looking for a perfect batard with a great ear and perfect oven spring here. This bread definitely has a personality of its own, and we'll let that shine.

---

300 grams wheat berry blend for 240 grams sifted bread flour

260 grams mixed whole grains

100 grams active sourdough starter

425 grams water, divided

11 grams kosher salt

FOR THE FLOUR: Mill the wheat berries as fine as you can and sift through a 50-mesh sifter. Measure out 240 grams of flour and place in a medium sized bowl. Save the wheat bran to coat the bottom of the dough after shaping.

Mill the mixed whole grains as fine as you can. Add this to the bowl with the sifted bread flour and mix well.

MIXING: In a large bowl with a lid, dissolve the sourdough starter in 414 grams of water. Add the flour and mix everything by hand until there is no more dry flour. Cover with the lid and rest for 1 hour. After resting for an hour, squeeze in the salt and remaining 11 grams of water until both are fully incorporated. Rest, covered, for 30 minutes.

BULK FERMENTATION: After resting for 30 minutes, give the dough one round of stretch and folds. Repeat this step twice more. After the last stretch and fold, bulk fermentation will last 2 to 2½ more hours until the dough has risen by about 50 percent and feels airy. The dough should remain covered the entire time.

PRESHAPE: Remove the dough from the container onto an un-floured work surface. Using a bench knife, shape the dough into a round. Rest for 45 to 60 minutes until the dough is relaxed.

SHAPING: Place a couche or a heavy towel on a sheet pan so it can easily be transferred to the fridge and coat the couche with wheat bran.

Shape the dough into a batard. Place it seam side up on the couche and cover with wheat bran. Fold the remaining part of the towel over the dough to nestle it.

PROOFING & BAKING: Proof the dough for 1 to 2 hours at room temperature until the dough has loosened and risen by about 20 percent before placing it in the fridge overnight.

The next day, set up your oven for steaming with lava rocks and preheat it to 500°F (260°C) for at least an hour to allow the stones to get nice and hot. Remove the dough from the fridge, and allow it to rest at room temperature while the oven preheats to get some of the chill off. When the dough is ready to bake, unfold the towel and gently lift the dough from underneath, placing it seam side up on a piece of parchment paper.

It's your call whether you score the dough or not. Baking seam side up allows the dough to expand naturally along the seams but can get still result in some strange blowouts. If you choose to score, just give it a couple of quick Xs—we're not looking for a sharp ear here.

Slide the parchment onto your pizza stone, and carefully pour boiling water over the lava rocks to create steam. Bake for 20 minutes, then remove the steam from the oven. Bake for 20 more minutes until the bread is a deep brown color and has a nice rustic look. When finished, place the loaf on a wire rack to cool for a couple of hours.

EXPLORING THE WONDERS
OF CORN

We all have those moments with food that change the way we perceive it and the way we eat. For instance, that heritage breed pork chop that tastes richer than anything from the grocery store; an apple from the farmers' market that is so sweet and delicious you sign up for a CSA on the spot; maybe a deeply colored loaf of artisan sourdough bread from a local bakery that makes you wonder how something so simple can be so complex.

I had this experience with a humble bowl of polenta—made from freshly-milled corn, of course. Polenta was a staple of my childhood that I never gave a second thought until then. How could it be so delicious? What was I missing? It was just cooked in water, with a small amount of butter and salt added at the end, yet it was so flavorful—and honestly like nothing I've tasted before. It all came from the fresh-milled corn. The flavor difference is far from subtle. This experience is what convinced me that I could never go back to store bought flour.

The aroma of corn being milled is one of my favorite smells, and it's ingrained in my memory after a trip to Janie's Mill just south of Chicago in Ashkum, Illinois. We make a quarterly trip to the mill so I can pick up whole grains and stoneground flours for my bakery. These trips are normally uneventful, but one day they were milling Bloody Butcher corn. As soon as they opened the door, the sweet, nutty, unmistakable smell hit me and blew my mind. Needless to say, I had to add a bag of Bloody Butcher to my order. That aroma will come through in the finished products as well, even with just a small amount of cornmeal added.

I'll be honest and admit that I don't find too much flavor difference between the varieties of corn. But the colors! To me there is no grain more beautiful than corn. It is not limited to the yellows and whites we are used to seeing. There are blue corns that range from a lighter shade to deep indigo; Bloody Butcher (my favorite name of any grain) with its intense purple-red; Wapsie Valley corn that looks like a sunburst guitar with yellows, burnt oranges and reds. I've seen Oaxacan green corn, and one called Glass Gem that has multicolored, opalescent kernels that vary from ear to ear.

Corn is a versatile grain for baking. It's more than just something to use to keep your English muffins from sticking. I often add a small amount of coarse milled cornmeal, about 1 to 2 percent of the flour weight, to my country sourdoughs, and it adds a nice aroma and texture. The recipes in this chapter will explore the various uses of freshly-milled corn in baking, from corn soakers to cornbread. Of course, we'll make that polenta that meant so much to me, and we'll use it in a couple of different loaves.

RYE & CORN BATARD

YIELDS ONE LOAF, ABOUT 750 GRAMS

This loaf of bread shows how adding just a little corn-meal can add so much to the texture and flavor. It's similar in technique to the country sourdoughs (pages 19 to 31), being around 30 percent whole grain, and it is a great starting point to understanding the wonders of corn. Cornmeal can take a lot of water, so there's a little extra added to this recipe to make sure the dough isn't too stiff. We're still looking for a nice, open crumb in this loaf. I occasionally make this bread for my weekly bread subscription service, and I get more compliments about it than any other bread I make.

325 grams wheat berry blend for 260 grams sifted bread flour

115 grams rye berries

8 grams whole corn kernels

76 grams active sourdough starter

314 grams water, divided

8 grams kosher salt

Wheat bran and rice flour mixture, for the basket (see page 12)

Wheat bran, for coating the bottom

FOR THE FLOUR: Mill the wheat berries as fine as you can and sift through a 50-mesh sifter. Measure out 260 grams of flour and place in a medium sized bowl. Save the wheat bran to coat the bottom of the dough after shaping.

Mill the rye berries as fine as possible and add to the bowl with the sifted flour.

Mill the corn kernels to a coarse consistency, add to the bowl with the other flours and mix well.

MIXING: In a large bowl with a lid, dissolve the sourdough starter in 306 grams of water. Add the flour and mix everything by hand until there is no more dry flour. Cover with the lid and rest for 1 hour. After resting for an hour, squeeze in the salt and the remaining 8 grams of water until both are fully incorporated. Rest, covered, for 30 minutes.

BULK FERMENTATION: After resting for 30 minutes, give the dough one round of stretch and folds. Repeat this step twice more. After the last stretch and fold, bulk fermentation will last 2 to 2½ more hours until the dough has risen by about 50 percent and feels airy. The dough should remain covered the entire time.

PRESHAPE: Remove the dough from the container onto an un-floured work surface. Using a bench knife, shape the dough into a round. Rest for 45 to 60 minutes until the dough is relaxed.

SHAPING: Line a proofing basket with a towel and coat with the wheat bran and rice flour mixture.

Shape the dough into a batard. Place it seam side up in the prepared basket, coat the bottom with wheat bran and cover the basket with a plastic bag.

PROOFING & BAKING: Proof the dough for 1 to 2 hours at room temperature until the dough has loosened and risen by about 20 percent before placing it in the fridge overnight.

The next day, place a Dutch oven in your oven and preheat to 500°F (260°C) for about an hour to make sure the Dutch oven is nice and hot. Remove the dough from the fridge, and allow it to rest at room temperature while the oven preheats to get some of the chill off. Score the dough and place it in the Dutch oven. Bake with the lid on for 20 minutes, then remove the lid and bake for 20 more minutes until it is dark and toasty. When finished, place the loaf on a wire rack to cool for a couple of hours.

DELI RYE WITH CARAWAY SEEDS

YIELDS ONE LOAF, ABOUT 800 GRAMS

This loaf of bread begs for a huge pile of pastrami and some spicy brown mustard. Growing up in New York City, it was always such a treat to hop on the subway and go to the classic Jewish delis like Katz's. The seeded ryes are what I remember most from those trips. They were always much more flavorful and crustier than the seeded rye I could buy from the grocery store, which seemed like nothing more than white bread with some coloring and caraway seeds. Every time I make this loaf, I'm transported back to the delis of my youth.

Here, we're using a technique where you add leftover bread soaked in some water to the dough. Any bread will do, but preferably use one with some rye. After making this bread, I like to save a slice or two in the freezer to use in future batches. It really does wonders for the texture of the crumb, making it moist and chewy.

FOR THE BREAD SOAKER

20 grams leftover bread

20 grams water

FOR THE DOUGH

415 grams wheat berry blend for 330 grams bread flour

60 grams rye berries

8 grams whole corn kernels

80 grams active sourdough starter

278 grams water

9 grams salt

7 grams caraway seeds

40 grams bread soaker

Wheat bran and rice flour mixture, for the basket (see page 12)

FOR THE BREAD SOAKER: In a medium bowl with a lid, crumble the leftover bread into crumbs. Pour the water over the crumbs and mix well. Cover the bowl and allow it to rest for at least 4 hours for the breadcrumbs to absorb the water.

FOR THE FLOUR: Mill the wheat berries as fine as you can and sift through a 50-mesh sifter. Save the wheat bran to coat the bottom of the dough after shaping. Measure out 330 grams of flour and place in a medium sized bowl.

Mill the rye berries as fine as possible and add to the bowl with the sifted flour.

Mill the corn kernels to a coarse consistency, then add them to the bowl with the other flours and mix well.

MIXING: In large bowl with a lid, dissolve the sourdough starter in the water. Add the salt, caraway seeds and the bread soaker, and then mix well. Add the flour and mix everything by hand until there is no more dry flour. Cover with the lid and rest for 1 hour.

BULK FERMENTATION: After resting for an hour, give the dough one round of stretch and folds. Allow to rest for 30 minutes and perform another set of stretch and folds. Repeat this step twice more for a total of four stretch and folds. After the last stretch and fold, bulk fermentation will last 2 to 2½ more hours until the dough has risen by about 50 percent and feels airy. The dough should remain covered the entire time.

PRESHAPE: Remove the dough from the container onto an un-floured work surface. Using a bench knife, shape the dough into a round. Rest for 45 to 60 minutes until the dough is relaxed.

SHAPING: Line a proofing basket with a towel, and coat it with the wheat bran and rice flour mixture.

Shape the dough into a batard. Place it seam side up in the prepared basket, and cover the basket with a plastic bag.

PROOFING & BAKING: Proof the dough for 1 to 2 hours at room temperature until the dough has loosened and risen by about 20 percent before placing it in the fridge overnight.

The next day, place a Dutch oven in your oven and preheat to 500°F (260°C) for about an hour to make sure the Dutch oven is nice and hot. Remove the dough from the fridge, and allow it to rest at room temperature while the oven preheats to get some of the chill off. Score the dough with horizontal slashes, and place it in the Dutch oven. Bake with the lid on for 20 minutes, then remove the lid and bake for 20 more minutes until it is dark and crusty, and the aroma of caraway seeds fills the air. When finished, place the loaf on a wire rack to cool for a couple of hours.

TOASTED CORN MICHE

YIELDS ONE LARGE ROUND LOAF, ABOUT 1,100 GRAMS

This bread is a staple at many gatherings in our family. Whether it's the holidays or just dinner at a friend's house, this stunning loaf is large and meant to be shared. The large round dough is a great canvas for decorative scoring or stenciling. You can really get creative with it. Everyone will surely be impressed if you bring this along to Christmas dinner. Miche is traditionally made with high extraction flour so we're sifting our freshly-milled whole wheat and adding in a little rye for good measure. Toasting the corn before milling brings out wonderful buttery aromas and sweet flavors from the grain. Your house will smell like buttered popcorn after you mill the corn. I prefer an extra dark bake on this bread. I like to say that I bake it as dark as my soul. The contrast of the crunchy, caramelized crust with the creamy, sweet crumb can't be beat.

FOR THE TOASTED CORN SOAKER

55 grams whole corn kernels

55 grams warm water

FOR THE DOUGH

613 grams whole wheat berries for 490 grams sifted flour

10 grams rye berries

75 grams active sourdough starter

425 grams water, divided

11 grams kosher salt

110 grams toasted corn soaker

Cornmeal, for coating

FOR THE TOASTED CORN SOAKER: Preheat the oven to 350°F (177°C). Place the corn kernels on a sheet tray, and roast them in the oven for about 10 minutes until fragrant and golden brown. Allow the corn to cool, then mill it coarse. In a small bowl, use a spoon to mix 55 grams of the coarse cornmeal with 55 grams of warm water. Set aside for at least 4 hours and up to 12 hours, so the corn can absorb the water and soften.

FOR THE FLOUR: Mill the whole wheat berries as fine as you can. Sift through a 50-mesh sifter, saving the wheat bran for coating. Measure out 490 grams of the sifted whole wheat flour and place in a medium sized bowl. Mill the rye berries as fine as you can. Add the rye flour to the bowl with the wheat flour and mix well.

MIXING: In a large bowl with a lid, dissolve the sourdough starter in 415 grams of water. Add the flour and mix everything by hand until there is no more dry flour. Cover with the lid and rest for 1 hour. After resting for an hour, squeeze in the salt, the remaining 10 grams of water and all the toasted corn soaker. Rest, covered, for 30 minutes.

BULK FERMENTATION: After resting for 30 minutes, give the dough one round of stretch and folds. Repeat this step twice more. After the last stretch and fold, bulk fermentation will last 2 to 2½ more hours until the dough has risen by about 50 percent and feels thick and airy. The dough should remain covered the entire time.

PRESHAPE: Remove the dough from the container, place on an un-floured work surface and shape the dough into a round using a bench knife. Rest for 45 to 60 minutes until it has relaxed.

SHAPING: Line a proofing basket with a towel, and dust it with cornmeal.

On a lightly floured surface, shape the dough into a round, and place it seam side up in the basket. Cover the bottom of the loaf with wheat bran. Place a plastic bag around the basket to keep it covered.

PROOFING & BAKING: Proof the dough for 1 to 2 hours at room temperature until the dough has risen by about 20 percent, then place it in the fridge overnight.

The next day, place a Dutch oven in your oven and preheat to 500°F (260°C) for about an hour to make sure the Dutch oven is nice and hot. Meanwhile, remove the dough from the fridge, and allow it to rest at room temperature to loosen up while the oven preheats. Score the dough and place it in the Dutch oven. Lower the oven to 450°F (232°C). Bake with the lid on for 20 minutes, then remove the lid and bake for 30 more minutes. You want a deep, rich color on this one to really bring out that sweet corn flavor. When finished, place the loaf on a wire rack to cool for a couple of hours.

BLOODY BUTCHER POLENTA BOULE

YIELDS ONE LOAF, ABOUT 900 GRAMS

Here we are—the loaf that started my love affair with corn. Every experiment I've ever done with cornmeal started with that first smell of freshly-milled Bloody Butcher Corn. The red specks of the polenta really make for a beautiful crumb. This bread uses unenriched polenta made specifically for the recipe.

FOR THE POLENTA

100 grams whole Bloody Butcher corn kernels

300 grams water

Kosher salt

FOR THE DOUGH

380 grams wheat berry blend for 300 grams sifted bread flour

80 grams white wheat berries

76 grams active sourdough starter

285 grams water, divided

8 grams kosher salt

150 grams cooked polenta

Cornmeal for coating

FOR THE POLENTA: Mill the Bloody Butcher corn kernels to a coarse consistency. In a medium pot, combine the cornmeal and water. Bring the mixture to a boil over high heat, stirring constantly. Turn the heat to low and simmer, stirring occasionally until the mixture is thick and creamy, about 45 minutes. Season lightly with salt. Allow the polenta to cool before using in the dough. The polenta can be made 3 days ahead of time. Store it in an airtight container in the fridge and bring to room temperature before using.

FOR THE FLOUR: Mill the wheat berries as fine as you can and sift through a 50-mesh sifter. Save the wheat bran to coat the bottom of the dough after shaping. Measure out 300 grams of flour and place in a medium sized bowl.

Mill the white wheat berries as fine as possible and add to the bowl with the sifted flour. Mix well.

MIXING: In a large bowl with a lid, dissolve the sourdough starter in 277 grams of water. Add the flour and mix everything by hand until there is no more dry flour. Cover with the lid and rest for 1 hour. After resting for an hour, squeeze in the salt, the remaining 8 grams of water and the cooked polenta. Rest, covered, for 30 minutes.

BULK FERMENTATION: After resting for 30 minutes, give the dough one round of stretch and folds. Repeat this step twice more for a total of three stretch and folds. After the last stretch and fold, bulk fermentation will last 2 to 2½ more hours until the dough has risen by about 50 percent and feels thick and airy. The dough should remain covered the entire time.

PRESHAPE: Remove the dough from the container, place on an un-floured work surface and shape the dough into a round using a bench knife. Rest for 45 to 60 minutes until it has relaxed.

SHAPING: Line a proofing basket with a towel, and dust it with cornmeal.

On a lightly floured surface, shape the dough into a round, and place it seam side up in the basket. Cover the bottom of the loaf with wheat bran. Place a plastic bag around the basket to keep it covered.

PROOFING & BAKING: Proof the dough for 1 to 2 hours at room temperature until the dough has risen by about 20 percent, then place it in the fridge overnight.

The next day, place a Dutch oven in your oven and preheat to 500°F (260°C) for about an hour to make sure the Dutch oven is nice and hot. Meanwhile, remove the dough from the fridge, and allow it to rest at room temperature to loosen up while the oven preheats. Score the dough and place it in the Dutch oven. Bake with the lid on for 20 minutes, then remove the lid and bake for 20 more minutes until the crust is dark and it smells like sweet, toasty corn. When finished, place the loaf on a wire rack to cool for a couple of hours.

SUNFLOWER POLENTA PAN LOAF

YIELDS ONE PAN LOAF, ABOUT 1,000 GRAMS

The inspiration for this bread came from a pretty unlikely source—school lunch. My daughter's school started serving sunflower seed butter & jelly sandwiches. The kids went wild for them, and there ended up being a shortage, so they were only around for about 2 weeks. So, we bought a jar of sunflower seed butter for home, and it blew my mind. It had such an intense toasted sunflower seed flavor, and my first thought was to use it in a bread, much like I use tahini in my sesame bread. I had some polenta in the fridge that I needed to use up and thought the combo of the intense sunflower seed would go great with the sweet corn.

I decided it would work best as a pan loaf to use for sunflower seed butter and jelly sandwiches—just to bring the whole thing together. It is super soft and moist, and just perfect for those sandwiches. Inspiration can truly come from anywhere.

---

350 grams wheat berry blend for 280 grams sifted bread flour

80 grams Yecora Rojo or another hard red wheat berry

40 grams rye berries

50 grams raw sunflower seeds

160 grams cooked polenta (see page 51)

50 grams sunflower seed butter

80 grams active sourdough starter

300 grams water, divided

9 grams kosher salt

Raw sunflower seeds for topping

FOR THE FLOUR: Mill the wheat berries as fine as you can and sift through a 50-mesh sifter. Measure out 280 grams of flour and place in a large bowl.

In a medium bowl, mix the Yecora Rojo and rye berries, then mill them as fine as possible and add to the bowl with the sifted flour. Mix well.

FOR THE POLENTA: Preheat the oven to 350°F (177°C). Place the raw sunflower seeds on a sheet tray, and roast them for about 10 minutes until golden brown. Allow to cool.

In a small bowl, combine the toasted sunflower seeds, the cooked polenta and the sunflower seed butter. Mix well and set aside.

MIXING: In a large bowl with a lid, dissolve the sourdough starter in 291 grams of water. Add the flour and mix everything by hand until there is no more dry flour. Cover with the lid and rest for 1 hour. After resting for an hour squeeze in the salt, the remaining 9 grams of water and the sunflower polenta mixture. Rest, covered, for 30 minutes.

BULK FERMENTATION: After resting for 30 minutes, give the dough one round of stretch and folds. Repeat this step twice more for a total of three stretch and folds. After the last stretch and fold, bulk fermentation will last 2 to 2½ more hours until the dough has risen by about 50 percent and feels thick and airy. The dough should remain covered the entire time.

PRESHAPE: Remove the dough from the container, place it on an un-floured work surface and use a bench knife to shape the dough into a round. Rest for 45 to 60 minutes until it has relaxed. In the meantime, place the raw sunflower seeds in a large bowl. Fold a kitchen towel in half, wet it and wring it out so it is slightly moist. The shaped dough will be rolled on the towel to help the seeds adhere.

SHAPING: Lightly oil a 9 × 4 × 4–inch (23 × 10 × 10–cm) Pullman pan.

Lightly flour a work surface, and shape the dough into a log. Roll the top of the dough on the wet towel then place it, seam side up, in the bowl with the sunflower seeds. Remove the dough from the bowl, and place it seam side down in the loaf pan. Cover it with a plastic bag.

PROOFING & BAKING: Proof the dough for 1 to 2 hours at room temperature until the dough has risen by about 20 percent, then place it in the fridge overnight.

The next day, set up your oven for steaming with lava rocks. Preheat the oven to 450°F (232°C). Meanwhile, remove the dough from the fridge so it can loosen up and get some of the chill off. The dough is ready to be baked when it has risen to just below the top of the pan.

Score the dough if desired, and place the pan in the oven and add steam. Lower the oven to 400°F (204°C) and bake for 20 minutes, then remove the steam and bake for an additional 25 minutes until the loaf has an internal temperature of at least 190°F (88°C) and the seeds are nicely toasted. When finished, place the loaf on a wire rack to cool for a couple of hours.

PEPITAS & GRITS WITH EINKORN FLOUR

YIELDS ONE LOAF, ABOUT 900 GRAMS

I love the earthy flavor of pepitas (shelled pumpkin seeds), especially when toasted. This bread was inspired by my friend in Louisville, Kentucky, who runs a small cottage bakery called El Bread (@el_breadshop). The bread community on Instagram is incredibly open and willing to share, and it's definitely made me a better baker.

And it's a good thing too, because this bread is one of my best sellers at the farmers' market. The golden pepitas on the top of the loaf are striking, and people can't resist.

I like the nutty, almost funky flavor of einkorn flour along with the earthy pepitas. I decided to use blue corn for the color it adds to the crumb, but feel free to use any corn you might have on hand. The bread will be delicious either way. When you remove it from the oven, the pepitas will start to snap, crackle and pop like Rice Krispies®.

FOR THE PEPITAS & GRITS

40 grams pepitas
40 grams whole blue corn kernels
80 grams boiling water

FOR THE DOUGH

400 grams wheat berry blend for 320 grams sifted bread flour
80 grams einkorn berries
80 grams active sourdough starter
308 grams water, divided
9 grams kosher salt
150 grams pepitas & grits
Raw pepitas for coating

FOR THE PEPITAS & GRITS: Preheat the oven to 350°F (177°C). Place the pepitas on a sheet tray and roast until golden brown and fragrant, about 10 minutes. Allow to cool.

Mill the blue corn to a coarse consistency and place in a medium bowl with a lid. Add the cooled pepitas and mix well. Carefully pour the boiling water over the mixture and stir until the cornmeal is well moistened. Cover and allow to soak for at least 4 hours for the cornmeal and seeds to absorb the water and soften.

FOR THE FLOUR: Mill 400 grams of the wheat berry blend as fine as you can. Sift through a 50-mesh sifter, saving the wheat bran for coating the shaped loaf. Measure out 320 grams of flour and place in a medium bowl.

Mill the einkorn berries as fine as you can. Add to the bowl with the sifted flour and mix well.

MIXING: In a large bowl with a lid, dissolve the sourdough starter in 300 grams of water. Add the flour and mix everything by hand until there is no more dry flour. Cover with the lid and rest for 1 hour. After resting for an hour, squeeze in the salt, the remaining 8 grams of water and all of the pepitas and grits mixture. Rest, covered, for 30 minutes.

BULK FERMENTATION: After resting for 30 minutes, give the dough one round of stretch and folds. Repeat this step twice more for a total of three stretch and folds. After the last stretch and fold, bulk fermentation will last 2 to 2½ more hours until the dough has risen by about 50 percent and feels thick and airy. The dough should remain covered the entire time.

PRESHAPE: Remove the dough from the container, place on an un-floured work surface and shape the dough into a round using a bench knife. Rest for 45 to 60 minutes until it has relaxed. In the meantime, place the raw pepitas in a large bowl. Fold a kitchen towel in half, wet it and wring it out so it is slightly moist. The shaped dough will be rolled on the towel to help the seeds adhere.

SHAPING: Line a proofing basket with a towel and lightly coat it with the dusting mixture.

Lightly flour a work surface and shape the dough into an oval. Roll the top of the dough on the wet towel then place it, damp side down, in the bowl with the pepitas. Remove the dough from the bowl, and place it seam side up in the proofing basket. Cover it with a plastic bag.

PROOFING & BAKING: Proof the dough for 1 to 2 hours at room temperature until the dough has risen by about 20 percent, then place it in the fridge overnight.

The next day, place a Dutch oven in your oven and preheat to 500°F (260°C) for about an hour to make sure the Dutch oven is nice and hot. Meanwhile, remove the dough from the fridge, and allow it to rest at room temperature to loosen up while the oven preheats. Score the dough, and place it in the Dutch oven. Bake with the lid on for 20 minutes, then remove the lid and bake for 20 more minutes. The pepitas should be a rich golden-brown color. When finished, place the loaf on a wire rack to cool for a couple of hours.

BUTTERMILK CORNBREAD

YIELDS ONE 10-INCH (25-CM) ROUND

This bread is the perfect example of how using fresh-milled corn can really elevate a simple dish to new heights. This just tastes and smells so intensely of corn. I like to use yellow corn in this bread for that classic cornbread look. Milled to a medium-fine consistency, it gives a nice texture from the coarser pieces and a good structure to the crumb from the corn that gets milled to a floury consistency. This is the beauty of stone milling.

I know using sugar in cornbread is a controversial subject. And you can certainly leave it out if you're a purist, but I think adding just a little brings out the sweetness in the corn and makes the bread's flavors pop.

I love the hint of pork flavor the lard gives to this cornbread, but you have to use fresh rendered lard here. The shelf stable stuff from the grocery store just won't cut it. You can find the fresh rendered lard at most Mexican markets as well as specialty butcher shops. Bacon fat would be an acceptable substitute but would also bring a smoky flavor along.

400 grams yellow corn kernels

7 grams kosher salt

3 grams baking soda

3 grams baking powder

20 grams sugar

420 grams full-fat buttermilk

2 large eggs

50 grams melted lard, divided

FOR THE CORNMEAL: Mill 400 grams of corn kernels to a medium-fine consistency and place in a large bowl. Add the salt, baking soda, baking powder and sugar to the bowl and mix well.

FOR THE BATTER: In a medium bowl, whisk together the buttermilk and eggs. Add the buttermilk mixture to the dry ingredients and mix well. Add 40 grams of the melted lard and mix until smooth. Set the batter aside while the oven preheats.

BAKING: Place a pizza stone in the middle of your oven, put a 10-inch (25-cm) cast-iron skillet on top and preheat the oven to 500°F (260°C) until the stone and skillet are very hot (about an hour).

Carefully remove the skillet from the oven, and add the remaining 10 grams of lard to coat the bottom of the pan. Add the cornbread batter to the skillet, and spread it evenly. Place the skillet back on the stone and bake for about 20 minutes until the cornbread is deeply browned and a toothpick inserted into the center comes out clean. When finished, allow the skillet and cornbread to cool for a couple of hours.

FRESH FLOUR
& FRIENDS

I get bored easily, and I think it shows in my baking. I'm constantly trying new ideas for bread just to keep things interesting for myself. And you know what? Most of the ideas work great.

At the farmers' market where I sell my bread, I try to offer different items every week. It's hard not to when you're standing among all the marvelous produce that the farmers bring to the market. I wasn't sure adding whole blueberries to a dough would produce a good loaf of bread, but I tried it anyway, and it has become one of my all-time favorites.

In this chapter, we're going to pair our freshly-milled flours with some of their best friends. From classics like Sesame Semolina (page 60) and the Cinnamon Raisin Pan Loaf (page 63), to recipes I made up when I was thinking about writing this book like the Fig & Almond Batard with Ancient Grains (page 76), all these recipes have something added to the dough. The QR to the right links to a short video of how I like to incorporate add-ins.

METHOD FOR FOLDING IN INGREDIENTS

I hope making these recipes will inspire you to experiment with your baking. Try adding in your favorite ingredient—you might just find a new favorite.

SESAME SEMOLINA

YIELDS ONE LOAF, ABOUT 800 GRAMS

This sesame bread is one I've been chasing for as long as I can remember. I grew up in a predominantly Italian American neighborhood in Brooklyn with a ton of bakeries. One of my earliest bread memories is the bread my grandfather, who lived upstairs from us, would eat. The crust was a deep color and covered in sesame seeds. The crumb had a golden hue, probably from semolina flour. He didn't speak much English, and I didn't speak any Italian, so I was never able to find out which of the many bakeries he got it from.

This one comes pretty close to the bread from my memory but with a few twists. My goal was to amp up the sesame flavor of this loaf. I started by adding toasted sesame seeds, but that wasn't enough. Then one day, it hit me: what better way to get a toasted sesame flavor than tahini? The tahini also provides a nice softness to the crumb. I like to go for full coverage of seeds on the outside, both to add to that umami flavor and for texture. I mill the durum to a semolina consistency, which is classic, but Kamut or even a hard white wheat would work great. This bread is a flavor bomb, which is not something that can usually be said about a loaf of bread!

400 grams wheat berries for 320 grams sifted flour

80 grams durum berries

20 grams sesame seeds

10 grams tahini

9 grams kosher salt

328 grams water, divided

80 grams active sourdough starter

Wheat bran and rice flour mixture, for the basket (see page 12)

Raw sesame seeds, for coating

FOR THE FLOUR: Mill the wheat berries as fine as you can and sift through a 50-mesh sifter. Save the wheat bran for coating. Measure out 320 grams of flour, and place it in a medium sized bowl.

Mill the durum berries to the consistency of semolina, and add it to the bowl with the sifted wheat flour. Mix well.

FOR THE SESAME SEEDS: Preheat the oven to 350°F (177°C). Place the sesame seeds on a sheet tray and roast for about 10 minutes until they are fragrant and golden brown. Allow to cool. In a small bowl, mix the toasted sesame seeds with tahini, salt and 8 grams of water.

MIXING: In a large bowl with a lid, dissolve the sourdough starter in 320 grams of water. Add the flour and mix everything by hand until there is no more dry flour. Cover the bowl with a lid and rest for 1 hour. After resting for an hour, squeeze in the sesame seed mixture with the tahini and salt until fully incorporated. Rest, covered, for 30 minutes.

BULK FERMENTATION: After resting for 30 minutes, give the dough one round of stretch and folds. Repeat this step twice more for a total of three stretch and folds. After the last stretch and fold, bulk fermentation will last 2 to 2½ more hours until the dough has risen by about 50 percent and feels airy. The dough should remain covered the entire time.

PRESHAPE: Remove the dough from the container onto an un-floured work surface. Using a bench knife, shape the dough into a round. Rest for 45 to 60 minutes until the dough is relaxed. In the meantime, place the raw sesame seeds in a large bowl.

SHAPING: Line a proofing basket with a towel and coat with the wheat bran and rice flour mixture. Fold a kitchen towel in half, wet it and wring it out so it is slightly moist.

Lightly flour a work surface and shape the dough—I prefer an oval shape for this one. Roll the entire dough on the wet towel then place it in the bowl with the sesame seeds. Coat the whole thing, top and bottom, with the seeds. Place the dough seam side up in the basket and cover the basket with a plastic bag.

PROOFING & BAKING: Proof the dough for 1 to 2 hours at room temperature until the dough has loosened and risen by about 20 percent before placing it in the fridge overnight.

The next day, place a Dutch oven in your oven and preheat to 500°F (260°C) for about an hour to make sure the Dutch oven is nice and hot. Remove the dough from the fridge, and allow it to rest at room temperature while the oven preheats to get some of the chill off. Score the dough and place it in the Dutch oven. Bake with the lid on for 20 minutes, then remove the lid and bake for 20 more minutes until it is dark and toasty. When finished, place the loaf on a wire rack to cool for a couple of hours.

CINNAMON RAISIN PAN LOAF

YIELDS ONE PAN LOAF, ABOUT 1,150 GRAMS

This bread is my daughter's favorite and one she really likes to help out with. In fact, it's the first bread she's ever made from beginning to end. One day, during a break from school, she asked if we could bake some bread for a local community fridge. I said we could, but she would have to make it herself. She suggested we bake this cinnamon raisin bread, and we got to work. She milled, measured, mixed and shaped four loaves all by herself and I manned the oven. It was a very satisfying way to spend a day.

I like this bread with a hefty portion of whole wheat. I went with Red Fife which has a little spiciness of its own to play along with the cinnamon. There's a small amount of sugar to counteract the bitterness from the whole wheat and cinnamon, but it's not sweet by any means.

315 grams wheat berry blend for 250 grams sifted bread flour

250 grams Red Fife berries

125 grams active sourdough starter

11 grams kosher salt

5 grams sugar

400 grams water

125 grams raisins

5 grams ground cinnamon

FOR THE FLOUR: Mill the wheat berries as fine as you can and sift through a 50-mesh sifter. Measure out 250 grams of flour and place in a medium sized bowl.

Mill the Red Fife berries as fine as you can, and add them to the bowl with the sifted flour. Mix well.

MIXING AND BULK FERMENTATION: In a large bowl with a lid, dissolve the sourdough starter, salt and sugar in the water. Add the flour and mix everything by hand until there is no more dry flour. Cover with the lid and rest for 30 minutes.

After 30 minutes, perform the first set of stretch and folds, then cover again and rest 30 more minutes. Meanwhile, in a medium bowl, mix the raisins with the cinnamon.

During the second set of stretch and folds, add the raisin mixture. Place about a fifth of the mixture on the dough, fold over one side and add another fifth of the raisins; then, fold over another side and add another fifth of the raisins until you've folded all four sides and added all of the mixture. Rest for 30 minutes and perform one additional set of stretch and folds. Bulk fermentation will last about 4 more hours after the last stretch and fold until the dough has doubled and feels thick and airy.

PRESHAPE: Remove the dough from the container onto an un-floured work surface, and use a bench knife to shape the dough into a round. Rest for 45 to 60 minutes for the dough to relax.

SHAPING: Lightly oil a 9 × 4 × 4–inch (23 × 10 × 10–cm) Pullman pan.

On a lightly floured surface, shape the dough into a log. Place the dough seam side down in the prepared pan, and cover the pan with a plastic bag.

PROOFING & BAKING: Proof the dough for 1 to 2 hours at room temperature until the dough has risen by about 20 percent, then place it in the fridge overnight.

The next day, set up your oven for steam with lava rocks. Preheat the oven to 450°F (232°C). Meanwhile, remove the dough from the fridge so it can loosen up and get some of the chill off. Since the cinnamon can slow down fermentation a bit, the dough might need a little more proofing after the rest in the fridge. If so, leave it at room temperature until it has risen to just below the top of the pan.

Score the dough if desired, and place the pan in the oven. Carefully pour boiling water over the lava rocks to create steam. Lower the oven to 400°F (204°C) and bake for 20 minutes, remove the steam and bake for about 25 more minutes, until the loaf has an internal temperature of at least 190°F (88°C) and is nicely browned. When finished, place the loaf on a wire rack to cool for a couple of hours.

ROASTED WALNUT & APRICOT LOAF WITH EMMER FLOUR

YIELDS ONE LOAF, ABOUT 900 GRAMS

Walnuts are one of my favorite additions to a loaf of bread. They're delicious, healthy and add a great texture. Giving them a good roast in the oven before adding them to the dough really amps up their flavor as well. They're also incredibly versatile. Walnuts pair with any number of ingredients from cinnamon and raisins to olives (try it, it really works!), to my favorite, dried apricots. I like to use apricots that haven't been treated with sulfur rather than the bright orange ones that have been. Their flavor and texture is superior, and their darker, brownish color really pops in the crumb. It's really worth seeking them out, but if you can't find them, the sulfur treated apricots will work just fine.

Emmer is my grain of choice every time I use walnuts. The dark nuttiness of the ancient emmer grain is the perfect pairing to the nutty, almost bitter flavor of the roasted walnuts.

---

325 grams wheat berry blend for 260 grams sifted bread flour

115 grams emmer berries

75 grams walnuts

75 grams dried apricots, quartered

75 grams active sourdough starter

300 grams water, divided

8 grams kosher salt

Wheat bran and rice flour mixture, for the basket (see page 12)

Wheat bran, for coating the bottom

FOR THE FLOUR: Mill the wheat berries as fine as you can and sift through a 50-mesh sifter, saving the wheat bran for coating the bottom of the shaped dough. Measure out 260 grams of flour and place in a medium sized bowl.

Mill the emmer berries as fine as you can, and add them to the bowl with the sifted flour. Mix well.

FOR THE WALNUTS: Preheat the oven to 350°F (177°C). Place the walnuts on a sheet tray and roast for about 10 minutes until they are fragrant. Allow to cool. In a small bowl, mix these with the quartered apricots.

MIXING & BULK FERMENTATION: In a large bowl with a lid, dissolve the sourdough starter in 292 grams of water. Add the flour and mix everything by hand until there is no more dry flour. Cover with the lid and rest for 1 hour. After resting for an hour, squeeze in the salt and the remaining 8 grams of water. Rest, covered, for 30 minutes.

After resting the dough for 30 minutes, add about a fifth of the walnut mixture to the top of the dough, and perform the first round of stretch and folds, fold over one side and add another fifth of the mixture, folding over another side and adding another fifth of the mixture until you've folded all four sides and added all the walnuts and apricots.

Rest for 30 minutes and perform another series of stretch and folds. Repeat this step once more for a total of three stretch and folds. Bulk fermentation will last about 2½ to 3 hours after the last stretch and fold. Keep the dough covered the entire time. It is ready for the preshape when it has risen by about 50 percent and feels airy.

PRESHAPE: Remove the dough from the container onto an un-floured work surface, and use a bench knife to shape the dough into a round. Rest for 45 to 60 minutes for the dough to relax.

SHAPING: Line a proofing basket with a towel, and dust it with the wheat bran and rice flour mixture.

On a lightly floured surface, shape the dough into an oval, and place it seam side up in the basket. Coat the bottom of the dough with wheat bran. Cover the basket with a plastic bag.

PROOFING & BAKING: Proof the dough for 1 to 2 hours at room temperature until the dough has risen by about 20 percent, then place it in the fridge overnight.

The next day, place a Dutch oven in your oven and preheat to 500°F (260°C) for at least an hour so the Dutch oven will be nice and hot. Meanwhile, remove the dough from the fridge so it can loosen up and get some of the chill off. Score the dough, and place it in the Dutch oven. Bake with the lid on for 20 minutes, then remove the lid and bake for 20 more minutes. The bread is ready when it's a deep brown color and smells nutty and delicious. When finished, place the loaf on a wire rack to cool for a couple of hours.

TOASTED OAT PORRIDGE BOULE

YIELDS ONE LOAF, ABOUT 900 GRAMS

I grew up eating oatmeal every day for breakfast, and I hated it. It completely turned me off of eating breakfast for the rest of my life—until I came across a farmer at the market here in Oak Park who was selling a variety of whole grains and flours. I was just getting seriously into baking and had just purchased my first mill, so I was very excited to pick up just about everything she had to offer, including a bag of raw rolled oats. At this point, I hadn't had a bowl of oatmeal in 20 years, but I cooked some up to use in an oatmeal bread that I had wanted to try. It was a revelation. One bite of that oatmeal, and I was reminded of the difference quality ingredients can make. Unfortunately, I don't remember the name of the farm where I got the oats, and they haven't been back to the market since.

I like to use a high protein whole wheat, like Rouge de Bordeaux, in this bread. Porridges, especially oats, add a wonderful creaminess to the crumb, and the chew provided by the higher protein wheat fits just perfectly.

FOR THE OAT PORRIDGE

28 grams butter

80 grams rolled oats

160 grams water

10 grams maple syrup

FOR THE DOUGH

380 grams wheat berry blend for 300 grams sifted
   bread flour

100 grams Rouge de Bordeaux wheat berries

80 grams active sourdough starter

300 grams water, divided

9 grams kosher salt

160 grams oat porridge

Rolled oats for coating

FOR THE OAT PORRIDGE: In a medium saucepan, melt the butter over medium heat. Add the oats and stir to coat with the melted better. Cook, stirring constantly until the oats are a toasty brown color, about 5 minutes. Add 160 grams of water and bring to a boil. Reduce the heat to low and cook until the oats are thick and creamy, about 10 minutes. Remove the pan from the heat. Stir in the maple syrup and allow to cool.

FOR THE FLOUR: Mill the wheat berries as fine as you can and sift through a 50-mesh sifter. Save the wheat bran for coating. Measure out 300 grams of flour and place in a medium sized bowl.

Mill the Rouge de Bordeaux berries as fine as possible and add to the bowl with the sifted flour. Mix well.

MIXING: In a large bowl with a lid, dissolve the sourdough starter in 290 grams of water. Add the flour and mix everything by hand until there is no more dry flour. Cover with the lid and rest for 1 hour. After resting for an hour squeeze in the salt, the remaining 10 grams of water and all of the oat porridge. Rest, covered, for 30 minutes.

BULK FERMENTATION: After resting for 30 minutes, give the dough one round of stretch and folds. Repeat this step twice more for a total of three stretch and folds. After the last stretch and fold, bulk fermentation will last 2 to 2½ more hours until the dough has risen by about 50 percent and feels thick and airy. The dough should remain covered the entire time.

PRESHAPE: Remove the dough from the container, place it on an un-floured work surface and shape the dough into a round using a bench knife. Rest for 45 to 60 minutes until it has relaxed. In the meantime, place the rolled oats in a large bowl.

SHAPING: Line a proofing basket with a towel, and dust it with the dusting mixture. Fold a kitchen towel in half, wet it and wring it out so it is slightly moist. The shaped dough will be rolled on the towel to help the oats adhere.

On a lightly floured surface, shape the dough into a round. Place the dough on the damp towel and roll it around to moisten all the sides. Put the dough in the bowl with the oats and cover on all sides with oats. Place the dough seam side up in the proofing basket. Cover the basket with a plastic bag.

PROOFING & BAKING: Proof the dough for 1 to 2 hours at room temperature until the dough has risen by about 20 percent, then place it in the fridge overnight.

The next day, place a Dutch oven in your oven and preheat to 500°F (260°C) for about an hour to make sure the Dutch oven is nice and hot. Meanwhile, remove the dough from the fridge, and allow it to rest at room temperature to loosen up while the oven preheats. Score the dough, and place it in the Dutch oven. Bake with the lid on for 20 minutes, then remove the lid and bake for 20 more minutes until the oats are deeply browned. When finished, place the loaf on a wire rack to cool for a couple of hours.

BLUEBERRY RYE

YIELDS ONE LOAF, ABOUT 900 GRAMS

Every summer, my family and I head to Michigan to go blueberry picking. If you're anything like me, the novelty wears off after about 10 minutes and when your bucket is not even a quarter full. You push through in the hot August sun to fill the bucket and help your kids fill theirs. When you get home, you realize you have entirely too many blueberries and start trying to figure out what to do with all of them. That's how I came up with the recipe for this blueberry rye bread. I thought the sweetness of the blueberries would pair really well with the spiciness of the rye flour. Add in a little sugar and some butter, and it is almost like a blueberry muffin in bread form.

485 grams wheat berry blend for 385 grams sifted bread flour

96 grams rye berries

62 grams active sourdough starter

38 grams sugar

270 grams water

8 grams kosher salt

23 grams unsalted butter, room temperature

115 grams fresh blueberries

Wheat bran and rice flour mixture, for the basket (see page 12)

Wheat bran, for coating the bottom

FOR THE FLOUR: Mill the wheat berries as fine as you can and sift through a 50-mesh sifter, saving the wheat bran for coating the bottom of the shaped dough. Measure out 385 grams of flour and place in a medium sized bowl.

Mill the rye berries as fine as you can and add them to the bowl with the sifted flour. Mix well.

MIXING & BULK FERMENTATION: In a large bowl with a lid, dissolve the sourdough starter and sugar in the water. Add the flour and mix everything by hand until there is no more dry flour. Cover with the lid and rest for 30 minutes. After resting, squeeze in the salt and butter. Rest, covered, for 30 minutes.

After 30 minutes, perform the first set of stretch and folds. Cover again and rest for 30 more minutes. During the second set of stretch and folds, add the blueberries. Place about a fifth of the berries on the dough, fold over one side and add another fifth of the blueberries, folding over another side and adding another fifth of the blueberries until you've folded all four sides and added all the berries. Rest the dough for 30 minutes, and then gently perform one additional set of stretch and folds, taking care not to crush the blueberries. Bulk fermentation will last about 3 more hours after the last stretch and fold, until the dough has increased by about 50 percent and feels thick and airy.

PRESHAPE: Remove the dough from the container onto an un-floured work surface, and use a bench knife to shape the dough into a round. Rest for 45 to 60 minutes for the dough to relax.

SHAPING: Line a proofing basket with a towel, and dust it with the wheat bran and rice flour mixture.

On a lightly floured surface, gently shape the dough into a round, making sure not to burst the berries. Place it seam side up in the basket. Coat the bottom of the dough with wheat bran. Cover the basket with a plastic bag.

PROOFING & BAKING: Proof the dough for 1 to 2 hours at room temperature until the dough has risen by about 20 percent, then place it in the fridge overnight.

The next day, place a Dutch oven in your oven and pre-heat to 500°F (260°C) for at least an hour so the Dutch oven will be nice and hot. Meanwhile, remove the dough from the fridge so it can loosen up and get some of the chill off. Score the dough and place it in the Dutch oven. Lower the heat to 475°F (246°C). Bake with the lid on for 20 minutes, then remove the lid and bake for 20 more minutes. The bread will be a dark brown color and smell like a freshly-baked blueberry muffin. When finished, place the loaf on a wire rack to cool for a couple of hours.

GARLIC CONFIT, PARMESAN & BLACK PEPPER BATARD

YIELDS ONE LOAF, ABOUT 800 GRAMS

If there's one ingredient I can't live without, it has to be garlic confit. I always have a jar of it floating around my fridge. It is a simple way to add a ton of flavor to just about anything you're cooking. Just smash a clove right onto a slice of bread, and you've got instant garlic bread. That's basically what this bread is—built-in garlic bread. Adding some of the garlic oil from the confit really amps up the garlic flavor and adds a nice softness to the crumb. The butteriness of freshly-milled Kamut is the perfect pairing for the rich garlic, cheesy Parmesan and the bite from the black pepper.

FOR THE GARLIC CONFIT

1 head of garlic

1 cup (237 ml) extra virgin olive oil

1 sprig of fresh thyme

FOR THE DOUGH

360 grams wheat berry blend for 288 grams sifted bread flour

72 grams Kamut berries

72 grams active sourdough starter

288 grams water, divided

8 grams kosher salt

8 grams garlic oil (from garlic confit)

40 grams garlic confit

40 grams Parmesan cheese, shredded on the large holes of a box grater

4 grams cracked black pepper

Wheat bran and rice flour mixture, for the basket (see page 12)

Wheat bran, for coating the bottom

FOR THE GARLIC CONFIT: Separate the cloves of garlic from the head. Peel them and add them to a small saucepan. Cover the cloves with the extra virgin olive oil (depending on the size and shape of your pot you may need to add more oil to cover the garlic) and add the sprig of thyme. Heat over medium-low heat, stirring occasionally, for about an hour until the garlic cloves are browned and very soft. Store the confit in the refrigerator for up to three days.

FOR THE FLOUR: Mill the wheat berries as fine as you can and sift through a 50-mesh sifter, saving the wheat bran for coating the bottom of the shaped dough. Measure out 288 grams of flour and place in a medium sized bowl.

Mill the Kamut berries as fine as you can and add them to the bowl with the sifted flour. Mix well.

MIXING & BULK FERMENTATION: In a large bowl with a lid, dissolve the sourdough starter in 280 grams of water. Add the flour and mix everything by hand until there is no more dry flour. Cover with the lid and rest for 1 hour. After resting for an hour, squeeze in the salt, garlic oil and the remaining 8 grams of water. Rest, covered, for 30 minutes.

In a medium bowl, combine the garlic confit, shredded Parmesan and cracked black pepper. The garlic will be very soft and will break up a bit. That is okay.

After resting the dough for 30 minutes, add about a fifth of the garlic and cheese mixture to the top of the dough and perform the first round of stretch and folds, fold over one side and add another fifth of the mixture, folding over another side and adding another fifth of the mixture until you've folded all four sides and added all the garlic mixture.

Rest for 30 minutes and perform another series of stretch and folds. Repeat this step once more for a total of three stretch and folds. Bulk fermentation will last about 2½ to 3 hours after the last stretch and fold. Keep the dough covered the entire time. It is ready for preshape when it has risen by about 50 percent and feels airy.

PRESHAPE: Remove the dough from the container onto an un-floured work surface, and use a bench knife to shape the dough into a round. Rest for 45 to 60 minutes for the dough to relax.

SHAPING: Line a proofing basket with a towel and dust with the wheat bran and rice flour mixture.

On a lightly floured surface, shape the dough into an oval, and place it seam side up in the basket. Coat the bottom of the dough with wheat bran. Cover the basket with a plastic bag.

PROOFING & BAKING: Proof the dough for 1 to 2 hours at room temperature until the dough has risen by about 20 percent, then place it in the fridge overnight.

The next day, place a Dutch oven in your oven and preheat to 500°F (260°C) for at least an hour so the Dutch oven will be nice and hot. Meanwhile, remove the dough from the fridge so it can loosen up and get some of the chill off. Score the dough and place it in the Dutch oven. Bake with the lid on for 20 minutes, then remove the lid and bake for 20 more minutes. When finished, place the loaf on a wire rack to cool for a couple of hours.

OLIVE, FRESH HERB & CITRUS ZEST BOULE WITH WHITE WHEAT

YIELDS ONE LOAF, ABOUT 900 GRAMS

My favorite thing about adding ingredients to bread is when they burst out of the score and get charred in the oven. This is especially true of olives. I'm known to yank those charred olives right out of the loaf and eat them straight from the oven. There's a wonderful contrast between the part of the olive that gets direct heat and chars and the part that is buried in the bread and is still soft. I like to use whole olives in my bread because I just love the way the giant pieces look in each slice, but chopped olives are great too if you want them more uniformly distributed. Thyme and rosemary are my go-to herbs in this one, but I think it would be great with sage or even tarragon. Any herbs will work, so long as they bring a ton of flavor to match up with the briny olive and the bright pop from the citrus zest. Using a mild white whole wheat like Pasayten really lets those flavors shine.

350 grams wheat berry blend for 280 grams sifted bread flour

120 grams Pasayten hard white wheat berries

80 grams active sourdough starter

320 grams water, divided

9 grams salt

120 grams pitted mixed olives

4 grams mixed fresh herbs, minced

Zest of one lemon

Zest of one orange

Wheat bran and rice flour mixture, for the basket (see page 12)

Wheat bran, for coating the bottom

FOR THE FLOUR: Mill the wheat berries as fine as you can and sift through a 50-mesh sifter, saving the wheat bran for coating the bottom of the shaped dough. Measure out 280 grams of flour and place in a medium sized bowl.

Mill the white wheat berries as fine as you can and add them to the bowl with the sifted flour. Mix well.

MIXING & BULK FERMENTATION: In a large bowl with a lid, dissolve the sourdough starter in 312 grams of water. Add the flour and mix everything by hand until there is no more dry flour. Cover with the lid and rest for 1 hour. After resting for an hour, squeeze in the salt and the remaining 8 grams of water. Rest, covered, for 30 minutes.

In a medium bowl, combine the olives, chopped herbs and citrus zests. Mix until the olives are well coated with the herbs and zest.

After resting the dough for 30 minutes, add about a fifth of the olive mixture to the top of the dough, and perform the first round of stretch and folds. Fold over one side and add another fifth of the olives, folding over another side and adding another fifth of the mixture until you've folded all four sides and added all the olive mixture.

Rest for 30 minutes and perform another series of stretch and folds. Repeat this step once more for a total of three stretch and folds. Bulk fermentation will last about 2½ to 3 hours after the last stretch and fold. Keep the dough covered the entire time. It is ready for preshaping when it has risen by about 50 percent and feels airy.

PRESHAPE: Remove the dough from the container onto an un-floured work surface, and use a bench knife to shape the dough into a round. Rest for 45 to 60 minutes for the dough to relax.

SHAPING: Line a proofing basket with a towel, and dust it with the wheat bran and rice flour mixture.

On a lightly floured surface, shape the dough into a round, and place it seam side up in the basket. Coat the bottom of the dough with wheat bran. Cover the basket with a plastic bag.

PROOFING & BAKING: Proof the dough for 1 to 2 hours at room temperature until the dough has risen by about 20 percent, then place it in the fridge overnight.

The next day, place a Dutch oven in your oven and preheat to 500°F (260°C) for at least an hour so the Dutch oven will be nice and hot. Meanwhile, remove the dough from the fridge so it can loosen up and get some of the chill off. Score the dough and place it in the Dutch oven. Bake with the lid on for 20 minutes, then remove the lid and bake for 20 more minutes. The bread is ready when it's a deep brown color and the olives that poke out of the top have some char. When finished place on a wire rack to cool for a couple of hours.

WILD RICE, ONION & CRANBERRY BOULE

YIELDS ONE LOAF, ABOUT 950 GRAMS

This bread screams Thanksgiving to me—it's like a built-in stuffing! My wife's family is from Minnesota, and a wild rice casserole with pheasant is a dish we have every year. I wanted to add some of that wild rice to a bread to be used for our stuffing. Cooking wild rice is a time-consuming process, so the recipe makes a large batch to enjoy with your dinner or as an addition to soups and salads. I went with a heavier portion of rye flour because the spiciness plays nicely with the earthiness of the wild rice and the cranberries. Even if you don't use this bread for stuffing, it is the perfect addition to any meal.

FOR THE WILD RICE

250 grams wild rice

1,000 grams water

4 grams kosher salt

FOR THE ONION

1 small onion

15 grams butter

Kosher salt

FOR THE DOUGH

350 grams wheat berry blend for 280 grams sifted bread flour

80 grams rye berries

40 grams Turkey Red wheat berries

80 grams active sourdough starter

300 grams water, divided

9 grams kosher salt

88 grams cooked wild rice

40 grams sauteed onion

40 grams cranberries

Wheat bran and rice flour mixture, for the basket (see page 12)

Wheat bran, for coating the bottom

FOR THE WILD RICE: Combine the wild rice, water and salt in a saucepan. Bring to a boil over high heat, cover, and lower the heat to medium-low. Simmer for about 45 minutes to an hour, until the rice is tender. Allow the rice to cool, and measure out 88 grams of wild rice, saving the rest for another use.

FOR THE ONION: Chop the onion into a small dice. Set a sauté pan over medium heat and put in the butter. When the butter has melted, add the onion and season with a touch of salt. Cook until the onion starts to sweat and turns translucent, about 5 minutes. Allow to cool and measure out 40 grams of onion.

FOR THE FLOUR: Mill the wheat berries as fine as you can and sift through a 50-mesh sifter, saving the wheat bran for coating the bottom of the shaped dough. Measure out 280 grams of flour and place in a large sized bowl.

In a medium bowl, mix the rye berries and Turkey Red wheat berries and mill as fine as you can. Add them to the bowl with the sifted flour. Mix well.

MIXING & BULK FERMENTATION: In a large bowl with a lid, dissolve the sourdough starter in 292 grams of water. Add the flour and mix everything by hand until there is no more dry flour. Cover with the lid and rest for 1 hour. After resting for an hour, squeeze in the salt and the remaining 8 grams of water. Rest, covered, for 30 minutes.

Combine the cooked wild rice, sauteed onion and cranberries in a small bowl. After resting the dough for 30 minutes, add about a fifth of the wild rice mixture to the top of the dough, and perform the first round of stretch and folds. Fold over one side and add another fifth of the mixture, then fold over another side and add another fifth of the mixture until you've folded all four sides and added all the wild rice mixture.

Rest for 30 minutes, and perform another series of stretch and folds. Repeat this step once more for a total of three stretch and folds. Bulk fermentation will last about 2½ to 3 hours after the last stretch and fold. Keep the dough covered the entire time. It is ready for preshaping when it has risen by about 50 percent and feels airy.

PRESHAPE: Remove the dough from the container onto an un-floured work surface, and use a bench knife to shape the dough into a round. Rest for 45 to 60 minutes to let the dough relax.

SHAPING: Line a proofing basket with a towel, and dust it with the wheat bran and rice flour mixture.

On a lightly floured surface, shape the dough into a round, and place it seam side up in the basket. Coat the bottom of the dough with wheat bran. Cover the basket with a plastic bag.

PROOFING & BAKING: Proof the dough for 1 to 2 hours at room temperature until the dough has risen by about 20 percent, then place it in the fridge overnight.

The next day, place a Dutch oven in your oven and preheat to 500°F (260°C) for at least an hour so the Dutch oven will be nice and hot. Meanwhile, remove the dough from the fridge so it can loosen up and get some of the chill off. Score the dough and place it in the Dutch oven. Bake with the lid on for 20 minutes, then remove the lid and bake for 20 more minutes. The bread is ready when it is a deep brown color and your whole house smells like Thanksgiving. When finished, place the loaf on a wire rack to cool for a couple of hours.

A NOTE ON STUFFING: *Being a bread baker, stuffing is the most important part of the meal to me. A technique I like to use is to roast a spatchcocked turkey directly on top of some thick slices of this bread. The bread will soak up all the turkey drippings and get nice and toasty on the bottom. Chop it up, add in your sausage and sauteed vegetables and throw it back in the oven for 30 minutes.*

FIG & ALMOND BATARD WITH ANCIENT GRAINS

YIELDS ONE LOAF, ABOUT 600 GRAMS

This loaf came about after having dinner at a friend's house with my family. My friend set out a wonderful charcuterie platter that included some dried figs and toasted almonds. My daughter proceeded to eat every last fig and almond she could get her hands on, leaving none for the rest of us. Instantly I knew I had to add some figs and almonds to a loaf of bread.

This is a hearty loaf with a ton of fruit and nuts and it's a little smaller, to increase the crust to crumb ratio. Adding the sliced almonds to the top is the icing on the cake.

---

160 grams wheat berry blend for 125 grams sifted bread flour

63 grams emmer berries

63 grams einkorn berries

50 grams raw whole almonds

50 grams dried mission figs

50 grams active sourdough starter

5 grams kosher salt

200 grams water

Sliced almonds, for coating

Wheat bran and rice flour mixture, for the basket (see page 12)

Wheat bran, for coating the bottom

FOR THE FLOUR: Mill the wheat berries as fine as you can and sift through a 50-mesh sifter. Measure out 125 grams of flour and place in a medium sized bowl, saving the wheat bran to coat the bottom of the loaf.

In a medium bowl, mix the emmer and einkorn berries, then mill them very fine. Add it to the bowl with the sifted wheat flour. Mix well.

FOR THE FIGS & ALMONDS: Preheat the oven to 350°F (177°C). Place the raw whole almonds on a sheet tray and roast for about 15 minutes until they are fragrant and when cut the inside is the color of a brown paper bag. Allow them to cool, then roughly chop. Place in a small bowl.

Roughly chop the figs and add them to the bowl with the chopped almonds. Mix well.

MIXING & BULK FERMENTATION: In a large bowl with a lid, dissolve the sourdough starter and salt in the water. Add the flour and mix everything by hand until there is no more dry flour. Cover with the lid and rest for 30 minutes.

After resting the dough for 30 minutes, add about a fifth of the fig and almond mixture to the top of the dough and perform the first round of stretch and folds. Fold over one side and add another fifth of the mixture, folding over another side and adding another fifth of the mixture until you've folded all four sides and added all the figs and almonds.

Rest for 30 minutes and perform another series of stretch and folds. Repeat this step once more for a total of three stretch and folds. Bulk fermentation will last about 2½ to 3 hours after the last stretch and fold. Keep the dough covered the entire time. It is ready for preshaping when it has risen by about 50 percent and feels airy.

PRESHAPE: Remove the dough from the container and place it onto an un-floured work surface. Use a bench knife to shape the dough into a round. Allow the dough to rest for 45 to 60 minutes. In the meantime, place the sliced almonds in a large bowl.

SHAPING: Line a proofing basket with a towel, and dust it with the wheat bran and rice flour mixture. Fold a kitchen towel in half, wet it and wring it out so it is slightly moist. On a lightly floured surface, shape the dough into a batard, roll on the towel and place seem side up into the bowl of almonds. Remove the dough from the bowl and place it seem side up in the basket. Coat the bottom of the dough with wheat bran. Cover the basket with a plastic bag.

PROOFING & BAKING: Proof the dough for 1 to 2 hours at room temperature until the dough has risen by about 20 percent, then place it in the fridge overnight.

The next day, place a Dutch oven in your oven and preheat to 500°F (260°C) for at least an hour so the Dutch oven will be nice and hot. Meanwhile, remove the dough from the fridge so it can loosen up and get some of the chill off. Score the dough and place it in the Dutch oven. Bake with the lid on for 20 minutes, then remove the lid and bake for 20 more minutes. The bread is ready when the almonds are a deep golden color. When finished, place the loaf on a wire rack to cool for a couple of hours.

DARK CHOCOLATE, DRIED CHERRY & TOASTED PISTACHIO

YIELDS ONE LOAF, ABOUT 900 GRAMS

This is Valentine's Day in bread form. I don't think the combination of dark chocolate and dried cherries can be beat. I initially made this bread as a Valentine's treat for my wife and daughter with the idea of using it for ice cream sandwiches. Something about eating ice cream in between two slices of bread really appealed to me. I didn't want the bread to be too sweet, and the cherries and chocolate add just enough. I planned on using pistachio ice cream, so I added pistachios to the bread as well.

The bread was a winner. The ice cream sandwich, not so much.

---

480 grams wheat berry blend for 380 grams sifted bread flour

40 grams dried cherries

40 grams dark chocolate

40 grams pistachios

76 grams active sourdough starter

11 grams cocoa powder

8 grams kosher salt

312 grams water

Wheat bran and rice flour mixture, for the basket (see page 12)

Wheat bran, for coating the bottom

FOR THE FLOUR: Mill the wheat berries as fine as you can and sift through a 50-mesh sifter. Measure out 380 grams of flour and place in a medium sized bowl, saving the wheat bran to coat the bottom of the loaf.

FOR THE CHOCOLATE, CHERRIES & PISTACHIOS: Place the cherries in a medium bowl and cover with hot tap water. Allow to rest for about an hour for the cherries to plump up. Drain the cherries and place them in a medium bowl. Save the soaking liquid because it is delicious.

Roughly chop the chocolate into bite-sized pieces, and place them in the bowl with the cherries.

Preheat the oven to 350°F (177°C). Place the pistachios on a sheet tray and roast for about 15 minutes until they are fragrant and golden. Allow the pistachios to cool, and add them to the bowl with the chocolate and cherries. Mix well.

MIXING & BULK FERMENTATION: In a large bowl with a lid, dissolve the sourdough starter, cocoa powder and salt in the water. Add the flour and mix everything by hand until there is no more dry flour. Cover with the lid and rest for 30 minutes.

After resting the dough for 30 minutes, add about a fifth of the chocolate, cherry, pistachio mixture to the top of the dough and perform the first round of stretch and folds. Fold over one side and add another fifth of the mixture, then fold over another side and add another fifth of the mixture until you've folded all four sides and added all the chocolate mixture.

Rest for 30 minutes and perform another series of stretch and folds. Repeat this step once more for a total of three stretch and folds. Bulk fermentation will last about 2½ to 3 hours after the last stretch and fold. Keep the dough covered the entire time. It is ready for preshaping when it has risen by about 50 percent and feels airy.

PRESHAPE: Remove the dough from the container onto an un-floured work surface and use a bench knife to shape the dough into a round. Allow the dough to rest for 45 to 60 minutes.

SHAPING: Line a proofing basket with a towel and dust with the wheat bran and rice flour mixture.

On a lightly floured surface, shape the dough into a round, and place it seam side up in the basket. Coat the bottom of the dough with wheat bran. Cover the basket with a plastic bag.

PROOFING & BAKING: Proof the dough for 1 to 2 hours at room temperature until the dough has risen by about 20 percent, then place it in the fridge overnight.

The next day, place a Dutch oven in your oven and preheat to 500°F (260°C) for at least an hour so the Dutch oven will be nice and hot. Meanwhile, remove the dough from the fridge so it can loosen up and get some of the chill off. Score the dough and place it in the Dutch oven. Bake with the lid on for 20 minutes, remove the lid and bake for 20 more minutes. It can be hard to tell if the bread is done based on color because the dough is dark to begin with. It should have an internal temperature of about 200°F (93°C). When finished, place the loaf on a wire rack to cool for a couple of hours.

SEEDED SPELT PAN LOAF

YIELDS ONE PAN LOAF, ABOUT 950 GRAMS

Seeds and spelt are a match made in heaven. The robust nuttiness of the whole spelt flour is perfect with the toasted seed flavor. Any combination of seeds will work here—just keep the total quantity the same. Chia or hemp would be a nice addition.

I like to coat the entire loaf in seeds before baking. It gives a wonderful, crunchy texture to the outside of the bread and brings a nice contrast to the softened seeds that have been baked into the bread. Be mindful of the top of the loaf during baking—burnt seeds taste terrible. If the top seems like it is browning too quickly, you can cover it with a piece of aluminum foil to slow it down.

FOR THE SEEDS

40 grams flax seeds

40 grams water

20 grams sesame seeds

20 grams pumpkin seeds

20 grams sunflower seeds

20 grams poppy seeds

FOR THE DOUGH

350 grams wheat berry blend for 280 grams sifted
  bread flour

120 grams spelt berries

80 grams active sourdough starter

300 grams water, divided

9 grams kosher salt

FOR COATING

30 grams raw sesame seeds

30 grams raw pumpkin seeds

30 grams raw sunflower seeds

30 grams poppy seeds

FOR THE SEEDS: Preheat the oven to 350°F (177°C).

In a large bowl with a lid, add the flax seeds and water. Mix well, cover and set aside.

Place the sesame, pumpkin and sunflower seeds on a sheet tray and place in the oven. Roast until the seeds are toasted and fragrant, about 10 to 15 minutes. Allow the seeds to cool.

Add the toasted seeds and the poppy seeds to the bowl with the flax seeds and mix well.

FOR THE FLOUR: Mill the wheat berries as fine as you can and sift through a 50-mesh sifter. Measure out 280 grams of flour and place in a medium sized bowl.

Mill the spelt berries as fine as you can, and add them to the bowl with the sifted flour. Mix well.

MIXING & BULK FERMENTATION: In a large bowl with a lid, dissolve the sourdough starter in 292 grams of water. Add the flour and mix everything by hand until there is no more dry flour. Cover with the lid and rest for 1 hour. After resting for an hour, squeeze in the salt and the remaining 8 grams of water. Rest, covered, for 30 minutes.

After resting the dough for 30 minutes, add about a fifth of the seed mixture to the top of the dough and perform the first round of stretch and folds. Fold over one side and add another fifth of the seeds, folding over another side and adding another fifth of the mixture until you've folded all four sides and added all the seeds.

Rest for 30 minutes and perform another series of stretch and folds. Repeat this step once more for a total of three stretch and folds.

Bulk fermentation will last about 2½ to 3 hours after the last stretch and fold. Keep the dough covered the entire time. It is ready for preshape when it has risen by about 50 percent and feels airy.

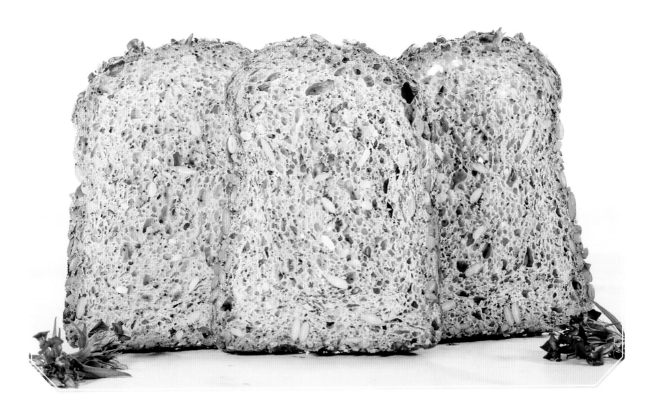

PRESHAPE: Remove the dough from the container onto an un-floured work surface, and use a bench knife to shape the dough into a round. Rest for 45 to 60 minutes for the dough to relax. In the meantime, add the seeds for coating to a large bowl.

SHAPING: Lightly oil a 9 × 4 × 4–inch (23 × 10 × 10–cm) Pullman pan. Fold a kitchen towel in half, wet it and wring it out so it is slightly moist.

On a lightly floured surface, shape the dough into a log. Roll the entire dough on the wet towel, then place it in the bowl with the seeds. Coat the whole thing, top and bottom, with the seeds. Place the dough seam side down in the prepared pan, and cover the pan with a plastic bag.

PROOFING & BAKING: Proof the dough for 1 to 2 hours at room temperature until the dough has risen by about 20 percent, then place it in the fridge overnight.

The next day, set up your oven to steam with lava rocks. Preheat the oven to 450°F (232°C). Meanwhile, remove the dough from the fridge so it can loosen up and get some of the chill off.

Score the dough, if desired, and place the pan in the oven. Carefully pour boiling water over the lava rocks to create steam. Lower the oven to 400°F (204°C) and bake for 20 minutes, release the steam and bake for an additional 25 minutes, until the loaf has an internal temperature of at least 190°F (88°C) and the seeds are nicely toasted. When finished, place the loaf on a wire rack to cool for a couple of hours.

FLATBREADS, PIZZAS & MORE

From baguettes to pizza, it never ceases to amaze me how varied and versatile rolls, buns and flatbreads can be.

A baguette is the perfect vehicle for a sandwich, but it's equally at home on a cheese plate or simply ripped apart and devoured.

Pizza allows for so much creativity—you can literally top it with anything, and it's going to be amazing.

In this chapter, we'll explore some of my favorite types of small breads, using doughs specific to each one. But there is a lot of flexibility in these recipes. If you're making a big batch of country sourdough and have a little dough left over, it can easily be turned into a fougasse. I do this all the time. It's a great way to experiment with different flavor combinations as well, since you're not committing the time and effort to make a dough, just using what's left over. I've come up with some of my favorite breads this way.

Many of the recipes in this chapter are for breads that people have strong opinions about. Ask anyone from New York about bagels, and you're in for an earful. I have the same passion about these breads, and I think that in adding fresh-milled flour and using sourdough, I've been able to achieve something that is both unique and traditional at the same time.

After all, baking is a personal experience and it's a joy to be able to take something you love and make it your own.

SOURDOUGH BAGUETTES

YIELDS TWO BAGUETTES, ABOUT 330 GRAMS EACH

That thin, crackly crust with a soft, creamy interior. You can't really beat a good baguette. Perfect for slicing up for a charcuterie plate or having a classic jambon-beurre. These baguettes are sure to satisfy.

The process takes a bit of practice. Figuring out how tight to shape them, transferring them from the proofing towel to the parchment with a board, scoring them so they open nice and evenly. These are all things that take time to master, but it's worth it. One difficulty with baking a baguette in a home oven is getting the right amount of steam. Baguettes need a lot of it, and our ovens aren't designed to hold steam. We're using the lava rocks method for this one, but remember to be careful when pouring the boiling water over the rocks. People have been known to shatter the glass on their oven door, so place a towel on the glass to help avoid this.

I don't like too much whole grain in my baguettes since I'm aiming for a lightness in the crumb. Just a little bit of spelt here will add a ton of nutty flavor and lend some extensibility to the dough, making it a bit easier to roll out.

395 grams of wheat berries for 315 grams sifted flour

35 grams of spelt berries

70 grams active sourdough starter

8 grams kosher salt

231 grams water

Rice flour, for coating

FOR THE FLOUR: Mill the wheat berries as fine as possible and sift through a 50-mesh sifter. Measure out 315 grams and place in a medium bowl, saving the wheat bran for dusting.

Mill the spelt berries as fine as you can, and add them to the bowl with the sifted flour. Mix well.

MIXING: In a large bowl with a lid, dissolve the sourdough starter and salt in the water. Add the flour and, using your hands, mix until there is no dry flour remaining. Cover the bowl and rest for an hour.

BULK FERMENTATION: After resting for an hour, remove the cover and perform the first set of stretch and folds. Cover the bowl and rest for 30 minutes. Repeat this step three more times for a total of four stretch and folds. Bulk fermentation will last about 2 hours after the last stretch and fold, until the dough is airy and has risen by about 50 percent. Place the covered bowl in the fridge overnight.

DIVIDING & PRESHAPE: Take the dough out of the fridge, and remove the dough from the bowl onto an unfloured work surface. Divide the dough into two pieces, about 330 grams each. Using a bench knife, shape the pieces into rounds and rest, covered with a towel, for an hour to allow the dough to relax.

SHAPING: Roll an edge of a flour sack towel or a couche to provide a place for the shaped baguettes to rest. Dust the towel with rice flour.

SHAPING METHOD FOR BAGUETTES

Working one piece at a time, turn the dough onto a lightly floured surface. Fold the top third of the dough toward the center. Press the seam and keep rolling the dough onto itself until it is a tight log. Using your palms, roll the dough out to about 16 inches (41 cm) in length. The amount of flour on your bench is crucial for this step. Too much flour and the dough will roll around like a limp noodle. Too little flour and the dough will stick to the bench.

Place the dough seam side up on the prepared towel, right up against the roll, and fold the towel up to create a divider for the next baguette. Repeat the prior shaping method with the other dough. Place it in the towel right up against the divider you created, and fold the remainder of the towel over the shaped doughs.

PROOFING: Proof the baguettes for about 6 to 8 hours at room temperature. They are ready to bake when the dough has just about doubled in size, and they are noticeably airy.

BAKING: Set up the oven for steaming with lava rocks and preheat it to 500°F (260°C) for at least an hour so the stone can get nice and hot.

Place a piece of parchment paper on a pizza peel.

Pull the fold in the towel apart so there is room between the two baguettes, lightly dust the bottoms with wheat bran. Using a board, flip one of the doughs from the towel to the board. Transfer the dough to the parchment paper. Repeat with the remaining baguette dough.

Score the baguette directly down the center, with three even slashes that slightly overlap. Slide the parchment onto the pizza stone and carefully pour boiling water over the lava rocks to create steam. Lower the oven to 450°F (232°C) and bake for 15 minutes, then remove the steam and bake 5 to 10 more minutes, until the bread is a deep golden brown. When finished, place the baguettes on a wire rack to cool for a couple of hours.

NEW YORK STYLE SOURDOUGH BAGELS

YIELDS SIX BAGELS, ABOUT 120 GRAMS EACH

As a native New Yorker, I have a lot of opinions about bagels. Not the least of which is that great bagels can be made anywhere. I don't buy into the myth of New York water being superior. Your local tap water will be just fine. In fact, since we're using fresh flour, I'll say that these bagels are more flavorful than anything you'll find in New York.

Bagels are usually made with a high gluten white flour. In place of that, we're using a strong wheat flour that has been sifted along with a little bit of whole rye flour, just for that added spiciness rye brings to the table.

The diastatic malt powder and malt syrup in the recipe are necessary for both that traditional bagel flavor as well as to help the bagels brown in the oven.

---

475 grams wheat berries for 380 grams sifted flour

20 grams rye berries

80 grams active sourdough starter

252 grams water

9 grams kosher salt

2 grams diastatic malt powder

2,000 grams water for boiling

80 grams malt syrup for boiling

FOR THE FLOUR: Mill the wheat berries as fine as you can and sift through a 50-mesh sifter. Measure out 380 grams of sifted flour and place in a medium bowl.

Mill the rye berries as fine as you can and add to the bowl with the sifted flour. Mix well.

MIXING: In a large bowl with a lid, dissolve the sourdough starter in the water. Add the salt and malt powder and mix well. Add the flour and mix with your hands until the mixture comes together and there is no more dry flour. Cover the bowl, and let it rest for an hour.

BULK FERMENTATION: After resting for an hour, perform the first set of stretch and folds. Cover the bowl and rest for 30 more minutes. Repeat this step three more times for a total of four stretch and folds. Bulk fermentation will last about 2 hours after the last stretch and fold. The dough should be airy and have risen by about 50 percent.

DIVIDING & PRESHAPE: Place a piece of parchment paper on a sheet tray, and lightly dust it with flour.

Remove the dough from the container, and place it on an un-floured work surface. Cut the dough into six pieces, each weighing about 120 grams. Shape them into rounds and place them on the floured parchment. Cover with a piece of plastic wrap and let rest for about 30 minutes for the dough to relax.

(continued)

New York Style Sourdough Bagels (Continued)

SHAPING METHOD FOR BAGELS

SHAPING & PROOFING: Remove the plastic wrap and dust the rounds with flour. With a sheet tray or a cutting board, press down on the rounds to flatten them. Then, using your thumb, indent each round in the middle. Pick up the dough and poke your thumb through the indentation, stretching the dough around in a circle before placing each piece back on the parchment. Repeat with the other five rounds.

Cover the sheet tray tightly with plastic wrap and allow to rest at room temperature for about an hour, until slightly risen, by about 10 percent. Place the sheet tray in the fridge overnight.

BOILING & BAKING: Place a pizza stone in the middle of your oven and preheat to 500°F (260°C) for at least an hour to get the stone nice and hot.

Remove the bagels from the fridge and allow to rest at room temperature while the oven is preheating and while you set up your boiling station.

In a pot large enough to hold three bagels, pour 2,000 grams of water. Dissolve the malt syrup in the water and bring to a boil over high heat.

Place the sheet tray with a rack near the pot to drain the bagels as they come out of the water.

If you're using toppings, place them in a medium bowl next to the sheet tray.

When the water is boiling, take one bagel dough at a time and drop it in the water. Repeat with two more bagel doughs. Gently stir to make sure the dough is not sticking to the bottom or sides of the pot. The bagels should float to the top of the water. Boil for about 30 seconds, flip them over and boil for 30 more seconds. Remove them from the pot and place on the rack. Let them drain for a minute and transfer to a piece of parchment paper. If you're topping them, then, while they are still damp, put one dough at a time in the bowl with the toppings and toss to completely cover the bagel before placing on the piece of parchment paper. Repeat the boiling process with the remaining three bagel doughs.

Using a pizza peel, slide the parchment with the bagel doughs onto the pizza stone. Bake the bagels for 20 to 25 minutes, until they're well browned. Check the bottoms of the bagels after about 15 minutes and if they are getting too dark place the bagels on a sheet tray for the remainder of the bake.

CHICAGO HOT DOG STYLE BAGEL TOPPING

I am pretty traditional when it comes to toppings on my bagels. I tend to stick with the classics—sesame, poppy, onion, everything. I'm not into flavors like honey lavender or ginger turmeric. It's a bagel, not a bar of soap. However, I've included one not-so-traditional topping that brings together my New York roots with my ties to Chicago. It's inspired by the Chicago style hot dog, but I think the flavors fit in with the usual bagel topping flavors.

30 grams poppy seeds
24 grams dried minced onion
10 grams celery seeds
6 grams mustard seeds
4 grams kosher salt

In a medium bowl, combine all the ingredients. The mixture can be stored in an airtight container in the pantry for months.

LARD BREAD

As far as I can tell this bread exists only in the neighborhood where I grew up, Bensonhurst in Brooklyn. There are similar breads out there—prosciutto bread and casatiello come to mind but they are not quite the same. Lard bread was a staple at every holiday for me growing up. Just another thing taken for granted until I found out that I couldn't find it anywhere after I moved away. So, I set out to make it myself, and my version comes pretty close to what I remember from my childhood. Of course, making it my own, I use freshly-milled flour and sourdough.

You'll want to use fresh rendered lard for the dough, not the shelf stable stuff from the grocery store. The types of meats can vary. I'll usually pick up whatever salami is on sale and a thick slice of prosciutto from the deli. I like sharp provolone for the cheese but Parmesan or pecorino could work well too.

This bread gets a pretty long bulk fermentation and a long proof, about 15 hours total, so timing it can be tricky. I like to start the dough in the evening and shape it right before bed to allow the dough to proof overnight and be ready to bake first thing in the morning.

---

440 grams wheat berry blend for 350 grams sifted
    bread flour

90 grams spelt berries

110 grams active sourdough starter

277 grams water

9 grams salt

22 grams fresh rendered lard

100 grams various cured meats, diced

50 grams sharp provolone, diced

3 grams coarsely ground black pepper

Wheat bran and rice flour mixture (see page 12)

FOR THE FLOUR: Mill the wheat berries as fine as you can and sift through a 50-mesh sifter, saving the wheat bran for coating the bottom of the shaped dough. Measure out 350 grams of flour and place in a medium sized bowl.

Mill the spelt berries as fine as you can and add them to the bowl with the sifted flour. Mix well.

MIXING & BULK FERMENTATION: In a large bowl with a lid, dissolve the sourdough starter in the 277 grams of water. Add the flour and mix everything by hand until there is no more dry flour. Cover with the lid and rest for 30 minutes. After resting, squeeze in the salt and the lard. Rest, covered, for 30 minutes.

Meanwhile, in a medium bowl, mix the cured meats, provolone and black pepper.

After 30 minutes, perform the first set of stretch and folds, cover again and rest for 30 more minutes. During the second set of stretch and folds, add the cured meats mixture. Place about a fifth of the mixture on the dough, fold over one side and add another fifth of the mixture, folding over another side and adding another fifth of the mixture until you've folded all four sides and added all the meats and cheese. Rest for 30 minutes and perform one additional set of stretch and folds. Bulk fermentation will last about 4 more hours after the last stretch and fold, until the dough has doubled in size and feels thick and airy.

DIVIDING & PRESHAPE: Remove the dough from the bowl onto an un-floured work surface. Divide the dough into 2 pieces, about 500 grams each. Using a bench knife, shape the pieces into rounds and rest, covered with a towel for an hour to allow the dough to relax.

SHAPING: Roll an edge of a flour sack towel to provide a place for the shaped doughs to rest. Dust the towel with the wheat bran and rice flour mixture.

Working one piece at a time, turn the dough onto a lightly floured surface. Fold the top third of the dough toward the center. Press the seam and keep rolling the dough onto itself until it is a tight log. Using your palms, roll the dough out to about 16 inches (41 cm) in length.

Place seam side up on the prepared towel, right up against the roll and fold the towel up to create a divider for the next baguette. Repeat shaping with the other dough. Place it in the towel right up against the divider you created and fold the remainder of the towel over the shaped doughs.

PROOFING: Proof the lard bread for about 8 hours at room temperature. They are ready to bake when the dough has just about doubled in size, and they are noticeably airy.

BAKING: Set up the oven for steaming with lava rocks and preheat it to 500°F (260°C) for at least an hour so the stone can get nice and hot.

Place a piece of parchment paper on a pizza peel.

Pull the fold in the towel apart so there is room between the two doughs and lightly dust the bottoms with wheat bran. Using a board flip one of the doughs from the towel to the board. Transfer the dough to the parchment paper. Repeat with the remaining dough.

Score the dough directly down the center, with three even slashes that slightly overlap. Slide the parchment onto the pizza stone and carefully pour boiling water over the lava rocks to create steam. Lower the heat to 450°F (232°C) and bake for 15 minutes, remove the steam and bake 5 to 10 more minutes, until the bread is a deep golden brown and smells heavenly.

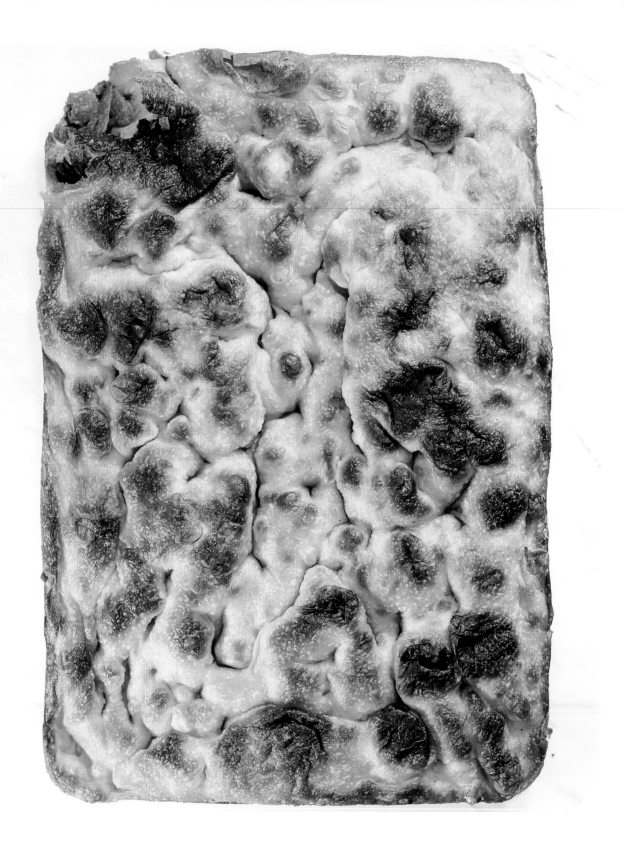

CLASSIC FOCACCIA WITH TWO VARIATIONS

YIELDS ONE FOCACCIA

Extra virgin olive oil is the first thing that comes to my mind when I think of focaccia. I do believe that after eating a slice, your hands should glisten with oil. Don't be shy with it here, and use a good one. I like Partanna®, a Sicilian olive oil that is available in grocery stores and doesn't cost an arm and a leg.

Focaccia is also the most relaxed dough to make. All you have to do is mix it, get it in the pan and let time do all the work. Edison white wheat from Camas Country Mill is a good choice here. It's strong enough to withstand the long proof and provides a super soft crumb.

---

625 grams Edison hard white wheat berries for 500 grams sifted flour

100 grams active sourdough starter

11 grams kosher salt

80 grams extra virgin olive oil, divided

425 grams water

Flaky sea salt

FOR THE FLOUR: Mill the Edison wheat berries as fine as you can and sift through a 50-mesh sifter. Measure out 500 grams and place in a medium bowl.

MIXING: In a large bowl with a lid, mix the sourdough starter, salt and 30 grams of extra virgin olive oil with the water. Add the flour and mix by hand until fully incorporated. Cover and rest for 30 minutes. After 30 minutes, perform the first set of stretch and folds. Repeat this step twice more for a total of three stretch and folds.

PROOFING: Oil a 13 × 9–inch (33 × 23–cm) pan with about 25 grams of olive oil.

After the last set of stretch and folds, immediately place the dough in the oiled pan. The dough may not entirely cover the bottom of the pan. That is okay—we will stretch the dough after proofing. Cover the pan, and allow the dough to proof at room temperature for 8 to 12 hours, until it is very light and airy.

TOPPING & BAKING: Place a pizza stone in the oven and preheat it to 500°F (260°C), for at least an hour until the stone is nice and hot.

If the dough has not entirely covered the pan, gently stretch the sides to the edges. Drizzle the remaining 25 grams of olive oil over top of the dough and, using your fingertips, dimple the dough all over. Sprinkle some flaky sea salt on the dough, and place it on the stone in the oven. Bake for about 30 minutes until the top is a deep brown.

FRESH TOMATO

Fresh tomatoes are the height of summer. Use a variety of types and colors here for a truly striking bread. It's important to get some liquid out of the tomatoes before adding them to the dough or else it will be a soupy mess.

A mix of tomatoes

Kosher salt

Extra virgin olive oil

1 proofed focaccia, see page 93

Flaky sea salt

FOR THE TOMATOES: Line a sheet tray with paper towels. Slice the tomatoes about ¼ inch (⅔ cm) thick and place on the towels. Lightly sprinkle the tomatoes with kosher salt, place some more paper towels over top and allow to rest while the oven preheats (about an hour).

TOPPING & BAKING: Place a pizza stone in the oven and preheat it to 500°F (260°C), for at least an hour until the stone is nice and hot.

Drizzle some olive oil over top of the dough and, using your fingertips, dimple the dough all over. Place the sliced tomatoes onto the dough, sprinkle on some flaky sea salt, and place it on the stone in the oven. Bake for about 30 minutes until the top is a deep brown and charred in spots.

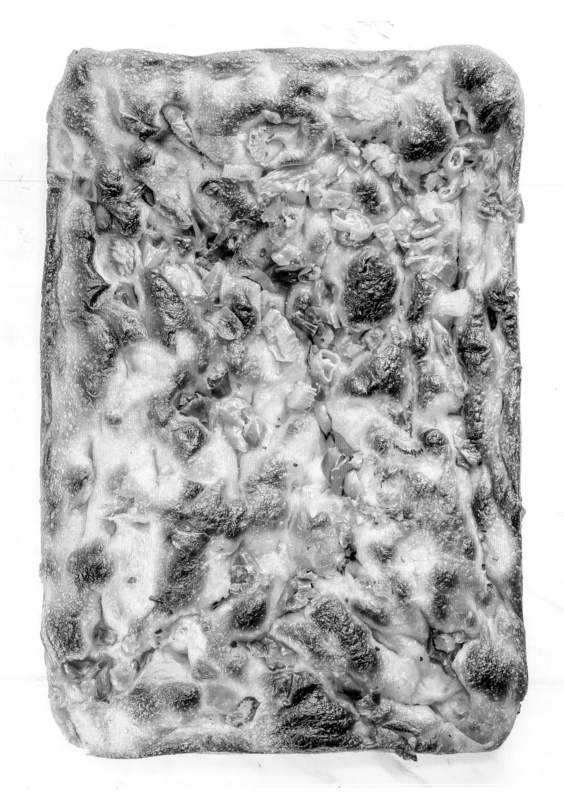

GIARDINIERA

Giardiniera is something I fell in love with after moving to the Chicago area. I'm never without a jar in the fridge. It's also a fun thing to make when you have an excess of produce in the summer. It lasts a long time and adds a great pop to anything you put it on.

Extra virgin olive oil
1 proofed focaccia, see page 93
½ cup (118 ml) giardiniera

TOPPING & BAKING: Place a pizza stone in the oven and preheat it to 500°F (260°C), for at least an hour until the stone is nice and hot.

Drizzle some olive oil over top of the dough and, using your fingertips, dimple the dough all over. Scatter the giardiniera over the top, and place on the stone in the oven. Bake for about 30 minutes until the top is a deep brown.

ZA'ATAR FLATBREAD

YIELDS SIX FLATBREADS, ABOUT 90 GRAMS EACH

These flatbreads are inspired by my friends at Hominy Farm (@hominyfarm), a wood-fired sourdough bakery located in Asheville, North Carolina. They make a flatbread topped with za'atar called manoushe. Za'atar is a Middle Eastern dried herb blend, with sesame seeds and sumac. You can find it in well-stocked grocery stores.

For the yogurt in the dough, you'll want to use a full fat one that is on the thinner side, not a Greek style yogurt. I've been making my own yogurt at home for as long as I've been baking bread, and I love when I can incorporate it into my baking. It will provide a softness and tenderness to this dough as well as acting as a browning agent.

I'll usually double this recipe when I make it, and when it comes time to divide it, I put half of the dough in the fridge to use over the next couple of days so I can have fresh flatbreads every day.

225 grams wheat berry blend for 180 grams bread flour

90 grams wheat berries

30 grams rye berries

120 grams water

90 grams plain whole milk yogurt

60 grams active sourdough starter

7 grams kosher salt

¼ cup (25 g) za'atar

¼ cup (50 g) extra virgin olive oil

FOR THE FLOUR: Mill the wheat berry blend as fine as you can and sift through a 50-mesh sifter. Measure out 180 grams of flour and add it to a large bowl.

In a medium bowl, mix the wheat and rye berries, mill them as fine as possible and add them to the bowl with the sifted bread flour.

MIXING: In a large bowl with a lid, mix the water with the yogurt. Dissolve the sourdough starter and salt in the mixture and, using your hands, mix in the flour until there is no dry flour remaining. Cover the bowl and rest for 1 hour.

BULK FERMENTATION: After resting for an hour, remove the cover and perform the first set of stretch and folds. Cover the bowl and rest for 30 minutes. Repeat this step three more times for a total of four stretch and folds. Bulk fermentation will last about 4 hours after the last stretch and fold, until the dough has doubled in size.

DIVIDING, SHAPING & BAKING: Place a pizza stone in the bottom third of your oven and preheat it to 500°F (260°C) for at least an hour until the stone is nice and hot.

In a small bowl, mix the za'atar with the extra virgin olive oil.

Remove the dough from the bowl and place on an unfloured surface. Divide the dough into six pieces, each weighing about 90 grams. Shape the dough into rounds and rest, covered with a towel, for about 20 minutes.

Line a pizza peel with a piece of parchment paper.

Lightly flour a work surface and, working one ball at a time, roll the dough into an 8 × 4–inch (20 × 10–cm) oval. If the dough is resisting, allow it to rest for a couple of minutes and continue rolling. Place the oval on the parchment paper and repeat with two more dough balls.

Spoon some of the za'atar mixture on each flatbread and slide the parchment into the oven. Bake for about 10 minutes, until the oil is bubbling and the dough is nicely browned.

Repeat the rolling and baking process with the remaining three dough balls.

FOUGASSE

A showstopper at the market, fougasse is always the first thing to go. It is incredibly versatile, and you can add pretty much anything to it, making it perfect to showcase seasonal ingredients. Add corn and poblano peppers in the heart of the summer, apples in the fall or whatever your heart desires.

It's also a flexible bread to make. You're not necessarily looking for a lot of oven spring or for an open crumb, which allows you to easily fit the dough into your schedule. Can't get around to shaping it on the day you made the dough? Throw it in the fridge for a day or two, and it'll be fine when you get to it. More often than not, I use scrap dough to make fougasse around here. I'll take whatever is left over, and if I want to add something to it, I'll do that during shaping. It always works out.

HERB, OLIVE OIL & SEA SALT

Herbs are a classic topping for fougasse, and any hearty herb will work here. I like thyme and rosemary, but sage or oregano could be fantastic as well. Fresh herbs are my preference whenever possible, but dried herbs work as well.

250 grams wheat berry blend for 200 grams sifted bread flour

40 grams active sourdough starter

4 grams kosher salt

160 grams water

Extra virgin olive oil

1 sprig thyme, leaves picked and chopped

1 sprig rosemary, leaves picked and chopped

Sea salt

Wheat bran and rice flour mixture (see page 12)

Wheat bran, for coating the bottom

FOR THE FLOUR: Mill the wheat berries as fine as possible and sift through a 50-mesh sifter. Measure out 200 grams of flour and place in a medium bowl, saving the wheat bran for dusting.

MIXING: In a large bowl with a lid, dissolve the sourdough starter and salt in the water. Add the flour and, using your hands, mix until there is no dry flour remaining. Cover the bowl and rest for an hour.

BULK FERMENTATION: After resting for an hour, remove the cover and perform the first set of stretch and folds. Cover the bowl and rest for 30 minutes. Repeat this step three more times for a total of four stretch and folds. Bulk fermentation will last about 2 hours after the last stretch and fold, until the dough is airy and has risen by about 50 percent.

PRESHAPE: Remove the dough from the container onto an un-floured work surface. Using a bench knife, shape the dough into a round. Rest for 45 to 60 minutes until the dough is relaxed.

FIRST SHAPE: If you're planning on making the fougasse in a leaf shape, line a proofing basket with a towel, and coat it with the wheat bran and rice flour mixture. Shape the dough into a round, and place it seam side up in the basket. Coat the bottom with wheat bran and cover the basket with a plastic bag. Allow to proof at room temperature for 1 to 2 hours until the dough has risen by about 20 percent, then place it in the fridge overnight.

If you're planning on making a long fougasse, place a towel on a sheet tray and fold up one end to provide a place for the dough to rest against. Coat the towel with the wheat bran and rice flour mixture. Shape the dough into a baguette shape, place on the towel seam side up and cover the bottom

with wheat bran. Fold the remainder of the towel over the dough to keep it in place. Cover the sheet tray with plastic, and allow the dough to proof for 1 to 2 hours until it has risen by about 20 percent, then place it in the fridge overnight.

FINAL SHAPE, TOPPING & BAKING: Set up the oven for steaming with lava rocks, and preheat it to 500°F (260°C) for at least an hour.

Place a piece of parchment paper on a pizza peel. Put the dough on the parchment and brush it with extra virgin olive oil. Sprinkle the herbs and sea salt over the top.

If you're making a leaf, use a bench knife to cut the dough in the middle. Stretch it into a triangle shape and make a few more cuts along the sides. Stretch out each cut.

If you're making a long fougasse, use a bench knife to make three even cuts along the length of the dough. Stretch each cut to provide ample space for the dough to expand.

Slide the parchment with the dough onto the hot stone, carefully pour boiling water over the lava rocks to create steam and bake for about 20 minutes until the fougasse is rich and brown.

SHAPING FOR
LEAF FOUGASSE

SHAPING FOR
LONG FOUGASSE

ROASTED CORN, POBLANO & JACK CHEESE

Corn epitomizes summer for me. We belong to a CSA from a local farm, and, starting in July, we get fresh corn literally every week for rest of the summer. It was only a matter of time before it started finding its way into some bread!

1 ear fresh corn, husk and silks discarded

Extra virgin olive oil

1 poblano pepper

80 grams pepper jack cheese, cubed

250 grams wheat berry blend for 200 grams sifted bread flour

40 grams active sourdough starter

4 grams kosher salt

160 grams water

Wheat bran and rice flour mixture (see page 12)

Wheat bran, for coating the bottom

FOR THE ROASTED CORN: Preheat the oven to 450°F (232°C). Place the corn on a sheet tray and coat it with olive oil. Roast the corn in the oven for about 15 minutes until it is slightly browned and sweet-smelling. Allow the corn to cool. Remove the kernels from the cob, and place them in a medium bowl.

FOR THE POBLANO PEPPER: Preheat the broiler to high. Place the poblano pepper on a sheet tray, and put it as close as possible to the broiler. Broil until the pepper is blackened on all sides and softened, about 5 minutes per side. Allow the pepper to cool, then remove the seeds. Chop the pepper into pieces about the same size as the corn kernels, and add it to the bowl with the corn. Add the cubed cheese to the bowl as well, and mix until evenly distributed.

FOR THE FLOUR: Mill the wheat berries as fine as possible and sift through a 50-mesh sifter. Measure out 200 grams of flour and place in a medium bowl, saving the wheat bran for dusting.

MIXING: In a large bowl with a lid, dissolve the sourdough starter and salt in the water. Add the flour and, using your hands, mix until there is no dry flour remaining. Cover the bowl and rest for 1 hour.

BULK FERMENTATION: After resting for an hour, add about a fifth of the corn mixture to the top of the dough and perform the first round of stretch and folds, fold over one side and add another fifth of the corn, folding over another side and adding another fifth of the mixture until you've folded all four sides and added all the corn mixture.

Rest 30 minutes and perform another series of stretch and folds. Repeat this step twice more for a total of four stretch and folds. Bulk fermentation will last about 2 hours after the last stretch and fold, until the dough is airy and has risen by about 50 percent.

PRESHAPE: Remove the dough from the container onto an un-floured work surface. Using a bench knife, shape the dough into a round. Rest for 45 to 60 minutes until the dough is relaxed.

FIRST SHAPE: If you're planning on making the fougasse in a leaf shape, line a proofing basket with a towel and coat with the wheat bran and rice flour mixture. Shape the dough into a round and place it seam side up in the basket. Coat the bottom with wheat bran, and cover the basket with a plastic bag. Allow to proof at room temperature for 1 to 2 hours until the dough has risen by about 20 percent, then place it in the fridge overnight.

If you're planning on making a long fougasse, place a towel on a sheet tray and fold up one end to provide a place for the dough to rest against. Coat the towel with the wheat bran and rice flour mixture. Shape the dough into a baguette shape, place on the towel seam side up and cover the bottom with wheat bran. Fold the remainder of the towel over the dough to keep it in place. Cover the sheet tray with plastic and allow the dough to proof for 1 to 2 hours until it has risen by about 20 percent, then place it in the fridge overnight.

FINAL SHAPE & BAKING: Set up the oven for steaming with lava rocks, and preheat it to 500°F (260°C) for at least an hour so the stone can get nice and hot.

Place a piece of parchment paper on a pizza peel.

If you're making a leaf, use a bench knife to cut the round dough right in the middle. Stretch it out into a triangle shape, and make a few more cuts along the sides. Stretch out each cut.

If you're making a long fougasse, use a bench knife to make three even cuts along the length of the dough. Stretch each cut to provide ample space for the dough to expand in the oven without the cuts closing.

Slide the parchment with the dough onto the hot stone, carefully pour boiling water over the lava rocks to create steam and bake for about 20 minutes until the fougasse is rich and brown.

APPLE FENNEL

I love apples, especially from the farmers' market. They just have so much complexity, and the variety always blows my mind. I like to use a mix of apples in this bread. Some of them will retain their shape and a little bite, while others will disappear completely, leaving behind a beautiful apple flavor. The anise flavor of the fennel almost makes this bread taste like an apple sausage.

250 grams wheat berry blend for 200 grams sifted bread flour

40 grams active sourdough starter

4 grams kosher salt

160 grams water

80 grams fresh apples, unpeeled, chopped

4 grams fennel seeds

Wheat bran and rice flour mixture (see page 12)

Wheat bran, for coating the bottom

FOR THE FLOUR: Mill the wheat berries as fine as possible and sift through a 50-mesh sifter. Measure out 200 grams and place in a medium bowl.

MIXING: In a large bowl with a lid, dissolve the sourdough starter and salt in the water. Add the flour and, using your hands, mix until there is no dry flour remaining. Cover the bowl and rest for an hour.

In a small bowl combine the apples and fennel seeds.

BULK FERMENTATION: After resting for an hour, add about a fifth of the apple mixture to the top of the dough, and perform the first round of stretch and folds. Fold over one side and add another fifth of the apple mixture, folding over another side and adding another fifth until you've folded all four sides and added all the mixture.

Rest for 30 minutes and perform another series of stretch and folds. Repeat this step twice more for a total of four stretch and folds. Bulk fermentation will last about 2 hours after the last stretch and fold, until the dough is airy and has risen by about 50 percent.

PRESHAPE: Remove the dough from the container onto an un-floured work surface. Using a bench knife, shape the dough into a round. Rest for 45 to 60 minutes until the dough is relaxed.

FIRST SHAPE: If you're planning on making the fougasse in a leaf shape, line a proofing basket with a towel and coat with the wheat bran and rice flour mixture. Shape the dough into a round, and place it seam side up in the basket. Coat the bottom with wheat bran, and cover the basket with a plastic bag. Allow the dough to proof at room temperature for 1 to 2 hours until it has risen by about 20 percent, then place it in the fridge overnight.

If you're planning on making a long fougasse, place a towel on a sheet tray and fold up one end to provide a place for the dough to rest. Coat the towel with the wheat bran and rice flour mixture. Shape the dough into a baguette shape, place on the towel seam side up and cover the bottom with wheat bran. Fold the remainder of the towel over the dough to keep it in place. Cover the sheet tray with plastic, and allow the dough to proof for 1 to 2 hours until it has risen by about 20 percent, then place it in the fridge overnight.

FINAL SHAPE & BAKING: Set up the oven for steaming with lava rocks, and preheat it to 500°F (260°C) for at least an hour so the stone can get nice and hot.

Place a piece of parchment paper on a pizza peel.

If you're making a leaf, use a bench knife to cut the round dough right in the middle. Stretch it out into a triangle shape, and make a few more cuts along the sides. Stretch out each cut.

If you're making a long fougasse, use a bench knife to make three even cuts along the length of the dough. Stretch each cut to provide ample space for the dough to expand in the oven without the cuts closing.

Slide the parchment with the dough onto the hot stone, carefully pour boiling water over the lava rocks to create steam and bake for about 20 minutes until the fougasse is rich and brown.

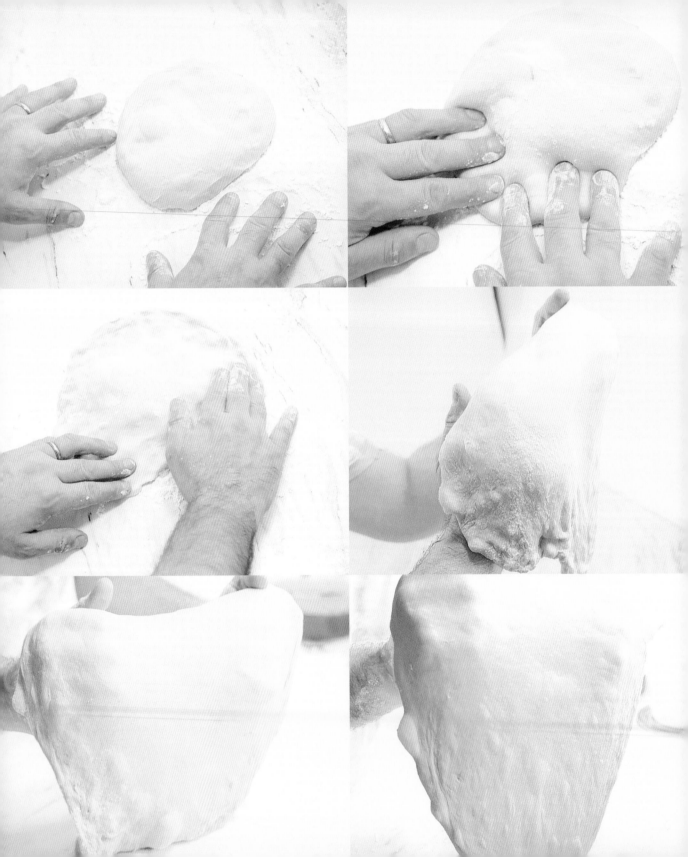

ALL-PURPOSE PIZZA DOUGH WITH TWO TOPPING VARIATIONS

YIELDS ONE PIZZA, APPROXIMATELY 14 INCHES (36 CM)

Homemade pizza is where it all started for me. I was a new father, and we had made the decision that I would quit my restaurant job and stay home with our daughter while my wife worked. We had pizza every Friday night, and it seemed like it would be more cost-effective if we could make it at home. Looking up pizza recipes on the internet led to the idea of sourdough pizza, and I've never looked back from there. This dough has been my go-to for some time now due its versatility and flavor. Kamut and durum flour add a wonderful flavor to the pizza, and their higher protein content gives a nice chew to the crust as well as making the dough nice and easy to handle.

225 grams wheat berry blend for 180 grams bread flour

10 grams Kamut berries

10 grams durum berries

40 grams active sourdough starter

5 grams kosher salt

4 grams extra virgin olive oil

2 grams sugar

128 grams water

FOR THE FLOUR: Mill the wheat berries as fine as you can and sift through a 50-mesh sifter. Measure out 180 grams of flour and place in a large bowl.

In a medium bowl, mix the Kamut and durum berries and mill to the consistency of fine semolina. Add to the bowl with the sifted bread flour and mix well.

MIXING: In a large bowl with a lid, dissolve the sourdough starter, salt, olive oil and sugar in the water. Add the flour and, using your hands, mix until all the flour is incorporated. Cover the bowl and rest for 30 minutes.

BULK FERMENTATION: After resting for 30 minutes, perform the first set of stretch and folds. Cover the bowl and rest for an additional 30 minutes. Repeat this step twice more for a total of three stretch and folds. Rest the dough an additional 30 minutes. Meanwhile, lightly oil a container with a lid.

BALLING THE DOUGH: After the 30-minute rest, remove the dough from the bowl and place it, smooth side down, on an un-floured work surface. Fold the four corners of the dough into the middle, flip it over and, using your hands, form the dough into a tight ball. Place the dough in the oiled container and place this into the fridge for at least a day (or up to 3 days). The dough will continue to ferment slowly in the fridge, which adds flavor.

It is ready to use when it has doubled in size.

CLASSIC CHEESE PIZZA

You can't beat a plain cheese pizza—it's an absolute classic. I've been chasing the perfect one since I moved from the East Coast to Chicagoland, where the pizza is a little bit different.

FOR THE SAUCE

1 28-oz can crushed tomatoes (I like 6 IN 1®)

20 grams tomato paste

12 grams extra virgin olive oil

3 grams dried oregano

10 grams granulated garlic

Pinch of crushed red pepper

Pinch of freshly ground black pepper

Kosher salt, to taste

Sugar, optional

FOR THE PIZZA

Proofed pizza dough (page 107)

Pecorino Romano, for grating

340 grams mozzarella cheese, shredded

FOR THE SAUCE: In a large bowl, combine all the ingredients. Season with salt to taste. Depending on the tomatoes, they may or may not need a little bit of sugar to round out the flavor. There will be some extra sauce if you're only making one pizza. It will keep for 3 days in an airtight container in the fridge.

SHAPING & BAKING THE PIZZA: Take the dough out of the fridge at least an hour before you plan to bake it, so it can warm up to room temperature. If the dough has not doubled in size, take it out of the fridge a little sooner.

Place a pizza stone in the bottom third of your oven and preheat it to 500°F (260°C) for at least an hour so the stone can get nice and hot.

Place the dough on a floured surface and, using your fingertips, press around the edges of the dough, flattening the edge but keeping the middle untouched. Lift the dough onto your knuckles and stretch the edges until the dough is approximately 14 inches (36 cm) in diameter. Place the dough on a piece of parchment. Spread about 200 grams of the tomato sauce over the stretched pizza dough. Grate some Pecorino Romano generously over the sauce. Top with the shredded mozzarella.

Slide the parchment with the pizza onto the pizza stone in the oven. Remove the parchment paper after about 4 minutes to keep it from burning.

Bake the pizza for an additional 6 to 10 minutes, until the crust is browned and the cheese and sauce are melted and bubbly. Depending on your oven, you may have to turn the broiler on to get the top of the pie done at the same time as the bottom. Grate more Pecorino Romano over the top of the finished pizza.

MORTADELLA & PISTACHIO

Mortadella and pistachios are something I always have on hand, so this pizza was a natural for me. With the mortadella added after the pizza comes out of the oven, it almost eats like a sandwich.

50 grams shelled roasted pistachios

50 grams extra virgin olive oil

Proofed pizza dough (page 107)

50 grams heavy cream

340 grams mozzarella cheese, shredded

5–6 slices mortadella

FOR THE PISTACHIOS: Place the pistachios in the bowl of a food processor. Process until coarsely chopped. With the motor running, drizzle in the olive oil. The mixture should still have coarse pieces of pistachios throughout.

SHAPING & BAKING THE PIZZA: Take the dough out of the fridge at least an hour before you plan to bake it, so it can warm up to room temperature. If the dough has not doubled in size, take it out of the fridge a little sooner.

Place a pizza stone in the bottom third of your oven and preheat it to 500°F (260°C) for at least an hour so the stone can get nice and hot.

Place the dough on a floured surface and, using your fingertips, press around the edges of the dough, flattening the edge but keeping the middle untouched. Lift the dough onto your knuckles and stretch the edges until the dough is approximately 14 inches (36 cm) in diameter. Place the dough on a piece of parchment. Spread the heavy cream over the stretched pizza dough. Top with the shredded mozzarella.

Slide the parchment with the pizza into the oven. Remove the parchment paper after about 4 minutes to keep it from burning.

Bake the pizza for an additional 3 to 7 minutes, until the crust is browned and the cheese and cream are melted and bubbly. Note that without tomato sauce, the pizza will cook more quickly. Depending on your oven, you may have to turn the broiler on to get the top of the pie done at the same time as the bottom. When the pizza is nicely browned, remove it from the oven and layer the mortadella slices over it, starting in the center. Drizzle with the pistachio oil mixture.

PAN PIZZA DOUGH + TWO TOPPING VARIATIONS

YIELDS ONE PAN PIZZA

I never liked pan pizzas as a kid. I always found them to be too doughy. I had no idea how light and airy they could truly be until I started making them myself. They are now my favorite. The timing of the dough is flexible since we're using the fridge for cold proofing, and I've found that parbaking the crust gives me the texture I am looking for, adding even more flexibility to the recipe. If the dough looks like it should be baked earlier than you were expecting, you can bake it and hold the parbaked crust at room temperature for a couple of hours.

220 grams wheat berry mix for 175 grams bread flour

25 grams Kamut berries

25 grams durum berries

25 grams Frederick wheat berries

180 grams water

50 grams active sourdough starter

6 grams kosher salt

20 grams extra virgin olive oil

FOR THE FLOUR: Mill the wheat berries as fine as you can and sift through a 50-mesh sifter. Measure out 175 grams of flour and add it to a large bowl.

In a medium bowl, mix the Kamut, durum and Frederick wheat berries, and mill them as fine as possible. Add them to the bowl with the sifted bread flour.

MIXING: In a large bowl with a lid, place the water and mix in the sourdough starter, salt and olive oil. Add the flour and, using your hands, mix until there is no dry flour remaining. Cover the bowl and rest for 30 minutes.

BULK FERMENTATION: After resting for 30 minutes, perform the first set of stretch and folds. Repeat this step twice more for a total of three stretch and folds. Allow the dough to increase in size by about 50 percent at room temperature—this will take approximately 2 hours after the last stretch and fold. Place the dough in the fridge, covered, for a day or two where it will continue to develop flavor.

SHAPING & PROOFING: On the morning you plan to make your pizza, heavily oil a 13 × 9–inch (33 × 23–cm) pan, preferably nonstick. Remove the dough from the fridge, and place it in the oiled pan. Press the dough with your hands to fill the pan. If the dough is resisting, allow it to rest for 5 minutes and press again. Repeat this as necessary. Don't worry if the dough does not reach all four edges—we'll be pressing it again just before baking. Cover the pan, and allow the dough to proof at room temperature until it is very airy and doubled in size, about 4 to 6 hours.

PARBAKING: Place a pizza stone in the bottom third of your oven, and preheat to 500°F (260°C) for at least an hour so the stone can get nice and hot.

Lightly oil your fingertips and dimple the dough all over, pressing it to the sides of the pan if necessary.

Place the pan with the dough on the stone and bake for about 10 minutes, until the dough is set and just starting to brown on the top. Remove it from the oven, place on a rack and allow to cool.

The parbaked dough is now ready to be topped and baked again.

PHILADELPHIA TOMATO PIE

These tomato pies are available at any number of bakeries and pizzerias in Philadelphia. Often served at room temperature, they make the perfect snack for the busy baker since they can be thrown together so easily. The tomatoes are the star here, so using a high-quality brand is important.

FOR THE SAUCE

1 28-oz can crushed tomatoes (I like 6 IN 1)

20 grams tomato paste

12 grams extra virgin olive oil

3 grams dried oregano

10 grams granulated garlic

Pinch crushed red pepper

Pinch freshly ground black pepper

Kosher salt, to taste

Sugar, optional

FOR THE PIZZA

Parbaked pizza crust (page 113)

Extra virgin olive oil, for drizzling

Pecorino Romano, for grating

FOR THE SAUCE: In a large bowl, combine all ingredients. Season with salt to taste. Depending on the tomatoes, they may or may not need a little bit of sugar to round out the flavor. There will be some extra sauce if you're only making one pizza. It will keep for 3 days in an airtight container in the fridge.

ASSEMBLING THE PIZZA: Flip the parbaked pizza crust so the bottom side is facing up. Drizzle some olive oil on the bottom of the crust and place it back in the pan, bottom side down.

Generously spread about 400 grams of tomato sauce over the crust. Drizzle with olive oil and grate some Pecorino Romano over the top.

Place the pizza in the oven on top of your pizza stone and bake for 20 minutes, until the bottom of the pie is well browned and the sauce is cooked and reduced a bit. Take the pizza out of the oven, grate more Pecorino Romano over the top and drizzle with more olive oil. Allow to cool to almost room temperature before eating.

POTATO, ROSEMARY & CREAM

I love this simple pizza and make it all the time, especially when potatoes are prevalent at the farmers' market. Any potato will do just fine, from starchy to waxy. They'll just give slightly different results. For a nice contrast, I like to use purple potatoes when I can get my hands on them. Don't skip the brining step—it will season the potatoes thoroughly and soften them a bit, ensuring that they're cooked at the end.

FOR THE POTATOES

12 grams salt
300 grams water
300 grams potatoes, thinly sliced

FOR THE PIZZA

Parbaked pizza crust (page 113)
Extra virgin olive oil, for drizzling
50 grams heavy cream
150 grams mozzarella, shredded
Leaves from 2 sprigs of rosemary
Pecorino Romano, for grating

FOR THE POTATOES: In a large bowl, dissolve the salt in the water. Place the sliced potatoes in the brine and allow to sit for about an hour. Drain well and place the potatoes on paper towels. Dry thoroughly.

ASSEMBLING THE PIZZA: Flip the parbaked pizza crust so the bottom side is facing up. Drizzle some olive oil on the bottom of the crust and place it back in the pan, bottom side down.

Shingle the potatoes on the crust, covering it completely. Drizzle the heavy cream over the potatoes and top with the shredded mozzarella, going completely to the edge so the cheese will create a crust along the side of the pan. Scatter the rosemary leaves over the cheese, grate some Pecorino Romano over the top and drizzle with some more olive oil.

Place the pizza in the oven, on top of your pizza stone and bake for 20 minutes, until the bottom of the pie is well browned, the cheese is melted, and the potatoes are browned. Depending on your oven, you may have to turn the broiler on halfway through to make sure the top and bottom finish at the same time. Take the pizza out of the oven, grate more Pecorino Romano over the top and drizzle with more olive oil.

LOFTY GOALS
Enriched Breads Using Commercial Yeast

I'm a sourdough baker. When I set out to learn about baking bread, I only wanted to use sourdough. If I found a recipe I wanted to make that used yeast, I would convert it to sourdough. I found this to be a great learning experience to see how sourdough would work with a variety of different doughs and to figure out how to make bread recipes my own.

That is, until I tried to tackle croissants. I thought it'd be a great challenge to make a sourdough croissant. It was, and I ended up with pretty good results after a couple of months of practice. But it just took so much time to proof the dough. Not having a proofer, I'd have to find a place to keep a tray of proofing croissants, covered so they wouldn't dry out, sometimes for a full 24 hours. At this point, I was hooked on croissant making, but the process was taking its toll, so I gave in and bought some commercial yeast.

And I'm really glad I did!

The proofing time for the croissants was cut from 24 hours to about 2 hours, which also allowed me to make a makeshift proofer in my oven. And honestly, the croissants went from being pretty good to exactly what I'm looking for.

This first foray into baking with yeast opened a whole new door for me. I started trying other yeasted recipes and found that not only can they be quick and easy but it's possible to add complexity to the breads with the use of pre-ferments like poolish and biga. And of course, since we're using fresh-milled flour, flavor isn't an issue at all, even for the quick breads.

All recipes in this chapter use SAF-Instant® Red yeast. The one-pound bags are easy to find online. I can even buy it at my grocery store. It costs about $6 and can be stored in an airtight container in the freezer for about a year without any loss of quality.

SOFT HONEY SANDWICH BREAD

YIELDS ONE LOAF, ABOUT 900 GRAMS

I bake this bread for my family more than any other. It's perfect for those grilled cheese and peanut butter and jelly sandwiches that seem to be the only thing my daughter will eat. Just slightly sweet from the honey and soft from the butter, it's a real treat.

It's simple and quick, about 4 to 5 hours from mixing to baking. But it is also incredibly flexible. If you need to slow it down at any point just throw the dough in the fridge. I'll often refrigerate after shaping to bake the following morning so the bread will be fresh for lunch.

600 grams wheat berry blend for 500 grams sifted bread flour

375 grams water

11 grams kosher salt

20 grams honey

7 grams SAF-Instant Red yeast

20 grams butter, softened

FOR THE FLOUR: Mill the wheat berries as fine as you can and sift through a 50-mesh sifter. Measure out 500 grams of flour and place in a bowl.

MIXING: In a large bowl with a lid, place the water, kosher salt, honey and yeast and whisk until combined. Add the flour and, using your hands, mix until fully incorporated. Cover and allow to rest for 20 minutes. After resting the dough, squeeze in the butter until fully incorporated. Cover the dough, and allow it to rest for 20 more minutes.

BULK FERMENTATION: After resting, perform the first set of stretch and folds. Cover the bowl and rest the dough for 20 minutes more minutes, repeating this step twice more for a total of three stretch and folds. Allow the dough to rest for another 1 to 1½ hours until double in size.

PRESHAPE: Place the dough on an un-floured surface and shape into a round. Allow to rest for 20 minutes. Meanwhile, lightly oil a 9 × 4 × 4–in (23 × 10 × 10–cm) Pullman pan.

SHAPING: On a lightly floured surface, shape the dough into a log and place seam side down in the prepared pan. Cover and proof for 1 to 2 hours until the dough is just peeking over the top of the pan.

BAKING: Set up your oven for steaming with lava rocks and preheat to 450°F (232°C) for about an hour. Place the Pullman pan on a sheet tray, score the dough if desired and place it in the oven. Carefully pour boiling water over the lava rocks to create steam, and lower the heat to 400°F (204°C). Bake for 20 minutes, then remove the steam and bake for 25 more minutes. If it seems like the top of the loaf is browning too quickly, you can lower the oven to 350°F (177°C). We're looking for a deep brown color on the top, and the finished bread should have an internal temperature of at least 190°F (88°C). When finished, place the loaf on a wire rack to cool for a couple of hours.

HONEY WHOLE WHEAT SANDWICH BREAD

YIELDS ONE LOAF, ABOUT 1,000 GRAMS

This is the same bread as the previous recipe except here we are not sifting the flour. To me, this is the perfect way to learn how different sifted and unsifted flour can be. This bread will be hearty and have a fuller flavor than the sifted version. However, the honey will temper the bitterness that can sometimes accompany whole wheat, and the butter will make this nice and soft, just as perfect for sandwiches as the sifted version.

550 grams wheat berry blend

412 grams water

12 grams kosher salt

22 grams honey

8 grams SAF-Instant Red yeast

22 grams butter, softened

FOR THE FLOUR: Mill the wheat berries as fine as you can and place in a bowl.

MIXING: In a large bowl with a lid, place the water, salt, honey and yeast and whisk until combined. Add the flour and, using your hands, mix until fully incorporated. Cover and allow the dough to rest for 20 minutes. After resting, squeeze in the butter until fully incorporated. Cover and rest for 20 more minutes.

BULK FERMENTATION: After resting, perform the first set of stretch and folds. Cover the bowl and rest for 20 more minutes, repeating this step twice more for a total of three stretch and folds. Allow the dough to rest for another 1 to 1½ hours until it has doubled in size.

PRESHAPE: Place the dough on an un-floured surface and shape into a round. Allow to rest for 20 minutes. Meanwhile, lightly oil a 9 × 4 × 4–in (23 × 10 × 10–cm) Pullman pan.

SHAPING: On a lightly floured surface, shape the dough into a log and place seam side down in the prepared pan. Cover and proof for 1 to 2 hours until the dough is just peeking over the top of the pan.

BAKING: Set up your oven for steaming with lava rocks and preheat to 450°F (232°C) for about an hour. Place the Pullman pan on a sheet tray, score the dough if desired and place in the oven. Carefully pour boiling water over the lava rocks to create steam, and lower the heat to 400°F (204°C). Bake for 20 minutes, then remove the steam and bake for 25 more minutes. If it seems like the top of the loaf is browning too quickly, you can lower the oven to 350°F (177°C). We're looking for a deep brown color on the top and the finished bread should have an internal temperature of at least 190°F (88°C). When finished, place the loaf on a wire rack to cool for a couple of hours.

POOLISH ENGLISH MUFFINS

YIELDS SIX MUFFINS, ABOUT 100 GRAMS EACH

My all-time favorite vehicle for breakfast sandwiches, I just can't get enough of these English muffins. They're a customer favorite as well, always sure to sell out quickly at the farmers' market. Using a poolish adds a nice complex flavor to these muffins. Using only real ingredients is really what sets them apart.

They'll last for a few days in a plastic bag on the counter, but they freeze beautifully. You can even split them before freezing and go straight from the freezer to the toaster.

---

440 grams wheat berry blend for 350 grams sifted bread flour, divided

262 grams water, divided

3 grams SAF-Instant Red yeast, divided

9 grams sugar

7 grams kosher salt

17 grams room temperature butter

Cornmeal for dusting

FOR THE FLOUR: Mill the wheat berries as fine as you can and sift through a 50-mesh sifter. Place in a medium bowl.

FOR THE POOLISH: In a medium size bowl with a lid, place 105 grams water. Measure out ⅛ teaspoon of the dry yeast and dissolve it in the water. Add 105 grams of the bread flour and, using a spoon, mix well until there is no dry flour. Let the poolish rest in a cool spot for 12 to 16 hours. It is ready to use when it has at least doubled and is bubbly on top.

FOR THE FINAL DOUGH: Place the remaining water in a large bowl with a lid. Add the remaining yeast, sugar, salt and poolish, and stir until dissolved. Add the rest of the flour and mix with your hands until there is no dry flour remaining. Cover the bowl and rest for 20 minutes. After 20 minutes, add the butter and mix well until the butter is incorporated. Cover and rest for 30 minutes.

BULK FERMENTATION: After 30 minutes has passed, uncover the bowl, and do the first round of stretch and folds. Repeat this step once more. The dough will ferment for about another hour after the last set of stretch and folds. It will be very airy and will have doubled in size.

DIVIDING, SHAPING & PROOFING: Dust a piece of parchment paper with cornmeal.

Place the dough on an un-floured work surface and divide it into six pieces of about 100 grams each. Form each piece into a round and place on the cornmeal-dusted parchment. Cover with a sheet of plastic wrap, and rest for 20 minutes to allow the dough to relax.

After 20 minutes, remove the plastic and dust the top of the rounds with cornmeal. Flip the rounds over so the seam side is facing up and, using a sheet tray or a cutting board, press down on the rounds to flatten them. Cover them with plastic wrap, and proof for about 2 hours until they are very airy and wobbly. We want to push the proof on these English muffins so they will not be dense inside.

BAKING: While the dough is proofing, place a pizza stone in the bottom third of the oven, and preheat it to 500°F (260°C) for at least an hour until the stone is nice and hot.

Using a pizza peel, slide the parchment onto the pizza stone. Bake for 5 minutes, then remove them from the oven and flip over each muffin. At this point, they'll look puffed up like burger buns, but they'll flatten when you flip them.

Slide them back into the oven to bake for about 5 more minutes. They're done when both sides are brown, and the internal temperature is 200°F (93°C). When finished, place the muffins on a wire rack to cool for a couple of hours.

SEEDED HOAGIE ROLLS WITH DURUM FLOUR

YIELDS SIX ROLLS, ABOUT 170 GRAMS EACH

I spent the early years of my adult life in Philadelphia, moving there just after college. I worked in a variety of restaurants and was pretty immersed in the food scene. One thing I can tell you about the city of Philadelphia is they know their sandwiches. I don't know if there is a better sandwich city around. Roast pork, cheesesteaks, chicken cutlets, Italian hoagies—they all rely on a great hoagie roll. That's one thing that I find lacking here in the Chicago area. So, I set out to make my own.

Of course, I wanted to use fresh-milled flour and decided that adding a little yeast would be beneficial. A hoagie roll needs to be nice and light inside to contrast the crisp crust. Whole durum flour was an obvious choice since I prefer a seeded roll, and durum and sesame are the perfect combination. The use of a biga and a cold bulk fermentation makes sure these hoagie rolls don't lack for flavor. I proof these on a couche like I do for baguettes, but proofing them seam side down on a parchment-lined sheet tray will work just as well.

600 grams wheat berry blend for 480 grams sifted bread flour, divided

120 grams durum berries

390 grams water, divided

6 grams SAF-Instant Red yeast, divided

6 grams sugar

12 grams kosher salt

12 grams extra virgin olive oil

Sesame seeds, for coating

Rice flour

FOR THE FLOUR: Mill the wheat berries as fine as you can. Sift through a 50-mesh strainer and into separate bowls, measure out 180 grams for the biga and 300 grams for the final dough.

Mill the durum berries to a fine consistency and add to the bowl with the flour for the final dough. Mix well.

FOR THE BIGA: In a medium size bowl with a lid, place 117 grams of water. Measure out ⅛ teaspoon of the dry yeast and dissolve it in the water. Add the 180 grams of sifted flour and mix well. Cover the bowl with a lid and allow to ferment at room temperature for about 8 hours, until doubled in volume.

FOR THE FINAL DOUGH: In a large bowl with a lid, place the remaining water, yeast, sugar, salt and olive oil. Stir to dissolve everything and add the biga one piece at a time, squeezing it in the water to dissolve. Add the remaining flour and using your hands, mix well until there is no dry flour remaining. Cover and rest 20 minutes.

BULK FERMENTATION: After 20 minutes has passed, uncover the bowl and do the first round of stretch and folds. Repeat this step twice more. After the last stretch and fold, place the bowl in the fridge overnight to finish bulk fermentation.

DIVIDING & PRESHAPE: The next morning, remove the dough from the bowl onto an un-floured work surface. Divide the dough into 6 pieces, about 170 grams each. Using a bench knife, shape the pieces into rounds and rest, covered with a towel, for an hour to allow the dough to relax. In the meantime, place the raw sesame seeds in a large bowl.

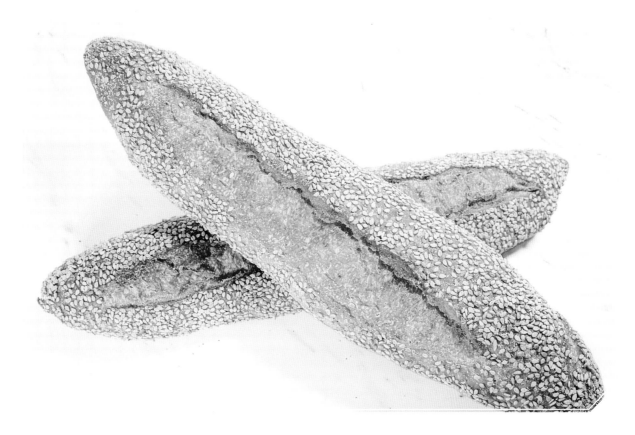

SHAPING: Roll an edge of a flour sack towel or a couche to provide a place for the shaped rolls to rest. Dust the towel with rice flour. Fold another kitchen towel in half, wet it and wring it out so it is slightly moist.

Working one piece at a time, turn the dough onto a lightly floured surface. Fold the top third of the dough toward the center. Press the seam and keep rolling the dough onto itself until it is a tight log. Using your palms roll the dough out to about 9 inches (23 cm) in length. Roll the entire dough on the wet towel then place it in the bowl with the sesame seeds. Coat the whole thing, top and bottom, with the seeds.

Place seam side up on the prepared towel, right up against the roll and fold the towel up to create a divider for the next piece of dough. Repeat shaping with the next piece of dough. Place it in the towel right up against the divider you created and repeat for the remaining rolls.

PROOFING: Proof the rolls for about 2 hours at room temperature. They are ready to bake when the dough has just about doubled in size, and they are noticeably airy.

BAKING: Set up the oven for steaming with lava rocks and preheat it to 500°F (260°C) for at least an hour so the stone can get nice and hot.

Place a piece of parchment paper on a pizza peel.

Pull the folds in the towel apart so there is room between the doughs. Using a board, flip one of the doughs from the towel to the board. Transfer the dough to the parchment paper. Repeat with the remaining dough.

Score the rolls and slide the parchment onto the pizza stone and carefully pour boiling water over the lava rocks to create steam. Lower the oven to 450°F (232°C) and bake for 15 minutes, remove the steam and bake 5 to 10 more minutes, until the bread is a deep golden brown and the sesame seeds are toasted and fragrant. When finished, place on a wire rack to cool for a couple of hours.

BUTTERY BURGER BUNS

YIELDS SIX BUNS, ABOUT 100 GRAMS EACH

Hamburgers are just about my favorite food. Not just beef either, I love a shrimp burger or one made from a sausage patty. The possibilities are endless really. The bun is so crucial to the burger and for the longest time burger buns were the one item I still bought at the grocery store. I just couldn't make a good one at home. Too dense, too crumbly, too distracting from the burger itself. Two things in this recipe solve these problems. First is allowing the dough to fully proof both in bulk and in final shape. This makes the buns super light and provides a solid base so the bun doesn't crumble when you bite into it.

The other is using the tangzhong method. This is a technique where you pre-gelatinize a portion of the flour in some of the liquid by cooking it into a paste. This provides a softness to the finished product that can't be matched.

We're using a soft white wheat, like Frederick or Sonora, for the whole wheat portion of the dough. This will bring the protein level of the bread down a little and make the buns less chewy than the stronger flour alone.

---

280 grams wheat berry blend for 225 grams sifted bread flour

75 grams Frederick wheat berries

180 grams whole milk, divided

2 large eggs, divided (1 whole egg for the dough and 1 for the egg wash)

30 grams sugar

6 grams kosher salt, plus a pinch for the egg wash

5 grams SAF-Instant Red yeast

60 grams butter, room temperature

Sesame seeds

FOR THE FLOUR: Mill the wheat berries as fine as you can and sift through a 50-mesh sifter. Measure out 225 grams of flour and place it in a medium bowl.

Mill the Frederick wheat berries as fine as possible and add to the bowl with the sifted bread flour. Mix well. Measure out 18 grams of the flour mixture and set it aside for the Tangzhong.

FOR THE TANGZHONG: In a small saucepan, bring 90 grams of milk to a simmer over medium heat. Add the 18 grams of flour, and whisk until the mixture is a thick paste. It'll take about a minute. Remove the mixture from the heat, place it into a large bowl with a lid and allow to cool to room temperature.

MIXING: Add the remaining 90 grams of milk, one egg, sugar, salt and yeast to the bowl with the tangzhong. Whisk until combined. Add the remaining flour and, using your hands, mix until the flour is incorporated. Cover the bowl and rest for 20 minutes. After resting, add about a quarter of the room temperature butter and mix with your hands until the butter is incorporated. Repeat until all the butter is used. Cover the bowl and allow to rest for 30 minutes.

BULK FERMENTATION: After resting for 30 minutes, perform the first set of stretch and folds. Repeat this step twice more for a total of three sets of stretch and folds. Rest covered until the dough is doubled in size, about 2 hours. Punch the dough down, and place the bowl in the fridge, covered, overnight.

DIVIDING AND SHAPING: The next morning, line a sheet tray with parchment paper and remove the bowl from the fridge. Place the dough on an un-floured work surface. Divide the dough into six pieces, each weighing about 100 grams. Using the palm of your hand, form the dough into balls. Place the balls on the parchment paper, cover with a towel and allow to rest for 20 minutes.

Dust the top of the dough balls with flour and, using a sheet tray or a cutting board, press the dough balls to flatten them. Cover with plastic wrap and allow to proof in a warm spot until doubled in size, about 4 hours.

BAKING: Set up your oven for steaming with lava rocks, and preheat the oven to 450°F (232°C).

Crack the egg for the egg wash into a small bowl, and add a splash of water and a pinch of salt. Whisk to combine.

Brush the tops of the buns with the egg wash and sprinkle sesame seeds over the top.

Carefully pour boiling water over the lava rocks to create steam, and place the buns on the middle rack. Lower the heat to 400°F (204°C), and bake until the buns are golden brown, about 20 minutes. When finished, place the buns on a wire rack to cool for a couple of hours.

CROISSANTS & VARIATIONS

YIELDS SIX CROISSANTS

For a long time, croissants were something I was reluctant to attempt at home. Just the idea of wrapping a block of butter in some dough and creating all those layers seemed so daunting. I have issues with straight lines, and croissants always seemed like they needed to be perfect. I learned that that isn't really true at all. Laminating the dough is a breeze, at least after you've done it a few times. And slightly askew croissants taste just as good as perfectly straight ones.

We're adding a lower-protein flour in with the soft red wheat here because it will help with the extensibility of the dough, making it much easier to roll out in a timely manner. One important thing to keep in mind when making croissants is that temperature is crucial. If the butter feels like it is getting too soft, it is best to pause and place the dough in the fridge to cool down a little.

If the dough is giving you problems and will not roll out easily, just let it rest for five minutes and come back to it. That resting period will allow it to relax a little, and it'll be more cooperative.

---

375 grams wheat berry blend for 300 grams sifted bread flour

90 grams soft red wheat berries for 70 grams sifted flour

115 grams cold water

115 grams cold whole milk

33 grams sugar

7 grams kosher salt, plus a pinch for the egg wash

5 grams SAF-Instant Red yeast

226 grams unsalted European style butter

1 egg for the egg wash

FOR THE FLOUR: Mill the wheat berries as fine as you can and sift through a 50-mesh sifter, measure out 300 grams and place in a medium bowl.

Mill the soft red wheat berries as fine and possible, sift through a 50-mesh sifter, measure out 70 grams and add to the bowl with the bread flour. Mix well.

FOR THE DOUGH: In a large bowl, place the water, milk, sugar, salt and yeast. Whisk to dissolve. Add the flour and, using your hands, mix until all the flour is hydrated and a stiff ball forms. Cover and allow to rest for about 5 minutes. After resting, knead the dough a few times until it forms a smooth ball. Loosely wrap the dough in plastic wrap, and place it in a plastic bag. Put the dough in the fridge for about 12 hours until doubled in size.

FOR THE BUTTER BLOCK: Place the butter on a piece of parchment paper. Using a rolling pin, beat the butter into a 6 × 6–inch (15 × 15–cm) square. Using a bench knife, clean up the edges of the square and scrape the top, trying to get it as smooth as possible. Fold the parchment over the butter block and wrap well in plastic wrap. Refrigerate until the dough is ready to use.

LAMINATING THE CROISSANTS: Remove the butter block from the fridge, and allow to sit at room temperature until it reaches a temperature of 50º to 57ºF (10º to 15ºC). This can happen quickly if it is warm in your kitchen.

Remove the dough from the fridge, and place it on a floured surface. Using a rolling pin, roll the dough into a 12 × 6–inch (30 × 15–cm) rectangle, double the size of the butter block in one direction. Place the butter in the center of the dough and fold up the sides so they meet in the middle, completely covering the butter.

(continued)

Croissants & Variations (Continued)

Making sure the dough and the surface are floured, roll the dough in one direction until it is about 20 inches by 8 inches (51 by 20 cm) long. Trim the edges so they are squared off. You can place the trimmings on the dough at this point so they can be folded back in. Brush off any excess flour, and fold the top side of the dough about two-thirds of the way down, then fold the bottom of the dough over the top, like folding a letter.

Turn the dough 90 degrees so you're rolling in the opposite direction, and roll the dough into a rectangle about 30 inches by 6 inches (76 by 15 cm). Trim the edges so they are square, saving the trim for a future use. Fold the top side of the dough about halfway down, brushing off any excess flour. Fold the bottom side of the dough right up the top side, then fold the whole thing in half, like closing a book. Wrap the dough tightly in plastic wrap and place in the fridge to rest for an hour.

SHAPING THE CROISSANTS: Make the egg wash by cracking an egg into a small bowl and whisking it with a pinch of salt and a splash of water.

Remove the dough from the fridge and place on a floured surface. Roll the dough into a rectangle about 10 inches wide by 12 inches long (25 by 30 cm). Trim the edges so they are neat, saving the trim for a future use. Cut the croissants into triangles with about a 4-inch (10-cm) base. Starting with the base of the triangle, roll them up into the classic croissant shape. Place them on a sheet tray lined with parchment paper. Brush each croissant with egg wash. Don't discard the egg wash just yet, as the croissants get another coat right before baking.

PROOFING & BAKING: Croissants like to proof in a warm, moist environment. I find using the oven with a bowl of boiling water to be the best substitute for a proofer. Place the tray of croissants in the oven (making sure not to turn it on, or all your hard work will be for nothing!), carefully pour some boiling water into a large bowl and place it in the bottom of the oven. The croissants will need to proof for 2½ to 3 hours, and you'll want to replace the water about every 45 minutes or so. The croissants are ready to bake when they have expanded significantly and are very wobbly. Remove the tray of croissants, along with the bowl of water, from the oven and preheat it to 425°F (218°C).

When the oven is preheated, brush the proofed croissants once more with the egg wash and place them in the center of the oven. Bake for 15 minutes at 425°F (218°C), lower the heat to 375°F (191°C), and bake for 10 to 15 more minutes until the croissants are a deep golden-brown color. If the bottoms seem like they're starting to burn, place another sheet tray under the one with the croissants.

Remove the croissants from the oven and place on a wire rack to cool.

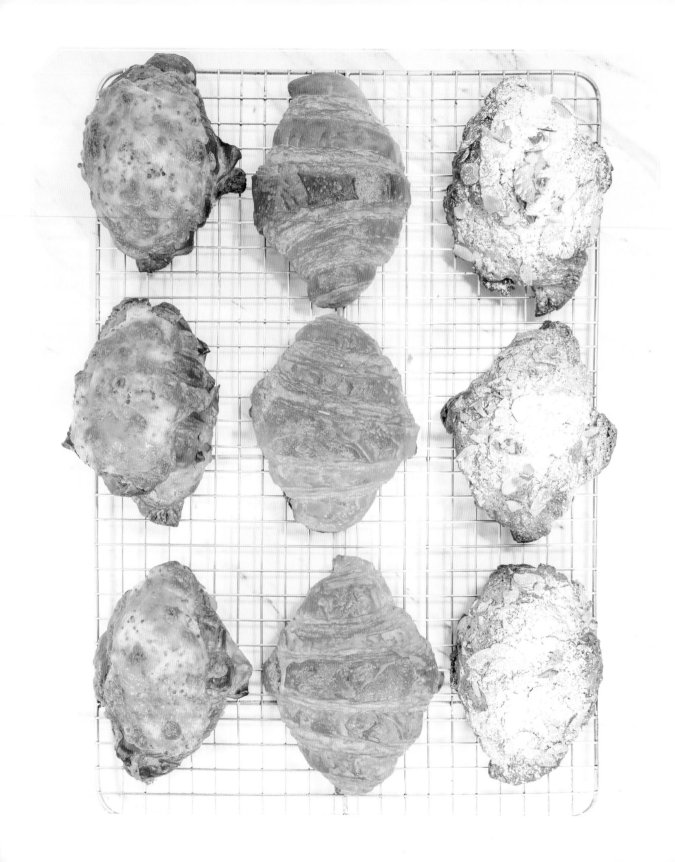

TWICE-BAKED HAM & CHEESE CROISSANTS

YIELDS SIX HAM & CHEESE CROISSANTS

This twice-baked ham and cheese croissant is one of my all-time favorite sandwiches. The creamy béchamel with a little bite from the mustard, the sweet, smoky ham and the sharp cheddar just work so well together. These are delicious at any temperature as well. Straight from the oven so you burn your mouth a little, cooled slightly just so they're still a little warm and the cheese is still gooey or even at a room temperature.

FOR THE MUSTARD BÉCHAMEL

20 grams butter
20 grams all-purpose flour
200 grams whole milk
30 grams whole grain mustard
Kosher salt
Freshly grated nutmeg
Freshly grated Pecorino Romano

FOR THE HAM & CHEESE CROISSANTS

6 croissants, day old
226 grams sharp cheddar cheese, shredded
6 slices of smoked ham
Mustard béchamel sauce

FOR THE MUSTARD BÉCHAMEL: In a medium saucepan, melt the butter over medium heat. Add the flour and whisk until smooth. Cook the butter and flour mixture for about a minute, stirring constantly, until it is a golden color.

Slowly add the milk to the saucepan, whisking constantly to prevent any lumps from forming. Bring the mixture to a boil, then lower the heat to low and simmer until the mixture is thick and creamy and will coat the back of a spoon.

Add the mustard to the milk mixture and stir to combine. Season to taste with salt, freshly-grated nutmeg and plenty of Pecorino Romano cheese.

Allow the béchamel to cool before using. It can be stored in the refrigerator for up to 3 days if you're not using it right away.

FOR THE HAM & CHEESE CROISSANTS: Preheat the oven to 425°F (218°C).

Split each croissant in half. Spread a tablespoon of the mustard béchamel on each side. Place some of the shredded cheese on the bottom half of each croissant and top the cheese with a slice of ham. Add a little more cheese on top of the ham and cover with the top of the croissant.

Top each croissant with some more of the béchamel, about half a tablespoon, and place more of the shredded cheddar on the béchamel so it sticks.

Place the assembled Ham & Cheese Croissants on a sheet tray lined with parchment paper. Bake in the oven until all the cheese is melted and the croissants are deep brown and crispy, about 25 minutes.

TOASTED ALMOND CROISSANTS

YIELDS SIX CROISSANTS

I love twice-baked croissants. Even more than fresh ones. Fresh croissants can be a bit delicate for me. A twice-baked croissant is anything but. Baked hard, maybe just a little burnt, and we've got something special.

Almond croissants have always been my favorite, and the simple step of toasting the almonds for the frangipane takes them to a whole new level. These take me back to my childhood and the Good Humor Toasted Almond ice cream bar. I wouldn't judge you if you wanted to split one of these open when it's still just a little warm and add a scoop of vanilla ice cream.

FOR THE TOASTED ALMOND FRANGIPANE

100 grams whole almonds

30 grams all-purpose flour

Pinch of kosher salt

113 grams butter, room temperature

53 grams brown sugar

1 large egg

FOR THE RUM SYRUP

60 grams dark rum

60 grams water

75 grams turbinado sugar

1 strip orange peel

FOR THE CROISSANTS

Sliced almonds

6-day-old croissants

Rum syrup

Toasted almond frangipane

Powdered sugar

FOR THE TOASTED ALMOND FRANGIPANE: Preheat the oven to 350°F (177°C).

Place the almonds on a sheet tray and roast until browned and fragrant, about 15 minutes. Allow them to cool to room temperature.

When the almonds are cool, place them in a food processor and pulse until finely ground. Place the almonds in a medium bowl, and add the flour and salt. Mix well and set aside.

Add the butter and brown sugar to the food processor, and process until light and fluffy. Add the egg and process until smooth. Add the almond flour mixture to the butter mixture, and process until smooth, about a minute.

The frangipane can be stored in the fridge for 3 days. Bring it to room temperature before using.

FOR THE RUM SYRUP: Combine all the ingredients in a small saucepan. Bring to a boil over medium heat, whisking to the dissolve the sugar. Discard the orange peel and cool to room temperature. The syrup can be refrigerated for up to a week.

FOR THE TOASTED ALMOND CROISSANTS: Preheat the oven to 425°F (218°C).

Place the sliced almonds in a medium bowl.

Split each croissant in half, brushing both cut sides generously with the rum syrup.

Scoop a heaping tablespoon of frangipane onto the bottom half of each croissant. Spread evenly across, using a little more frangipane if necessary. Close each croissant and place about a tablespoon more frangipane on the top of each one. Press the top of the croissant into the sliced almonds so they adhere to the frangipane.

Place the croissants on a sheet tray lined with parchment paper and bake for about 25 minutes, until the sliced almonds are toasted, the croissants are crispy and the frangipane is puffed. Dust with powdered sugar and cool on the wire rack.

CROISSANT SCRAP LOAF

YIELDS ONE PAN LOAF

When you make croissants, you're going to end up with a fair amount of scraps. Especially if you end up getting obsessed with making croissants, which is bound to happen. There's plenty you can do with the scraps such as baking them into their own little pastries topped with cheese or adding them into a new batch of dough to add some complexity to the flavor, but my favorite is baking them into a loaf of bread.

You'll need about 800 grams of scraps for this. I save all the trimmings in the freezer, and when I reach 800 grams, I'll make a loaf. As you get more practice rolling out the croissant dough, you'll end up with less trimming and you'll find yourself laminating a dough just to make this loaf of bread.

A lot of butter will escape from the dough when it's baking, essentially frying the bottom and sides in butter. Make sure to place the loaf pan on a sheet tray for this reason—they're not always watertight.

800 grams croissant scraps, defrosted if frozen
1 large egg for the egg wash
Kosher salt

SHAPING & PROOFING: Press the croissant scraps into a 9 × 9–inch (23 × 23–cm) rectangle. Roll them up into a log and place in a 9 × 4 × 4–inch (23 × 10 × 10–cm) Pullman pan.

Proof at room temperature until the dough is about half an inch from the top of the pan, about 5 hours.

BAKING: Preheat the oven to 450°F (232°C).

In a small bowl, whisk the egg with a pinch of salt and splash of water.

Brush the top of the proofed loaf with the egg wash.

Place the Pullman pan on a sheet tray and place in the middle of the oven. Lower the heat to 400°F (204°C) and bake for 40 minutes, until the loaf is golden brown. The internal temperature of the loaf should be at least 190°F (88°C).

APPLE TOAST

YIELDS EIGHT TOASTS

Move over French toast, this toast is the perfect brunch item. It can be assembled a day or two in advance with no trouble at all. Reminiscent of apple pie with the butter crust, crumb topping and sweet apples, this toast is sure to impress.

FOR THE APPLE SYRUP

120 grams apple cider
75 grams turbinado sugar

FOR THE CRUMB TOPPING

50 grams all-purpose flour
50 grams rolled oats
40 grams sliced almonds
45 grams brown sugar
Pinch of kosher salt
100 grams butter, melted

FOR THE TOAST

8 slices croissant scrap bread (page 137)
Apple syrup
Toasted almond frangipane (page 136)
Two apples, sliced
Crumb topping

FOR THE APPLE SYRUP: In a small saucepan, combine the apple cider and turbinado sugar. Bring to a boil over medium heat, whisking to the dissolve the sugar. Lower the heat to low, and simmer until the mixture is the consistency of a light syrup. Allow to cool. The mixture can be refrigerated for up to a week.

FOR THE CRUMB TOPPING: In a medium bowl, combine the flour, oats, almonds, brown sugar and salt, mixing well. Pour in the melted butter and, using your fingertips, mix until small clumps start to form. Set aside.

FOR THE TOAST: Preheat the oven to 425°F (218°C).

Place the sliced bread on a sheet tray lined with parchment paper. Generously brush each piece with the apple syrup. Scoop two tablespoons of toasted almond frangipane on each piece of bread, spreading it evenly. Fan four slices of apple in the center, and brush the apples with some of the apple syrup. Place the crumb topping around the edges, keeping the apples exposed.

Place in the oven and bake for 20 to 25 minutes, until the crumb topping is browned, the frangipane is puffed and the bottoms are well-toasted. Allow toast to cool on a wire rack.

ACKNOWLEDGMENTS

This book wouldn't be possible without the support of my family.

Thanks to my photographer, Josh Darr, for bringing the bread to life.

To my publisher, Page Street Publishing Co., for giving me the opportunity to write this book.

And special thanks to all my friends in the Instagram bread community for their inspiration and willingness to share their knowledge.

ABOUT THE AUTHOR

TIM GIUFFI is the owner and baker of Lyman Ave. Bread, a cottage bakery in Oak Park, Illinois, specializing in sourdough bread using freshly-milled whole grains. You can find him slinging his wares at the Oak Park Farmers' Market and biking around town on his bread bike.

INDEX